Sunshine Bill

by

W. H. G. Kingston

Sunshine bill
by W. H. G. Kingston

ISBN: 978-93-64289-85-6

Published by

DOUBLE 9 BOOKS

2/13-B, Ansari Road
Daryaganj, New Delhi – 110002
info@double9books.com
www.double9books.com
Tel. 011-40042856

ABOUT THE AUTHOR

William Henry Giles Kingston (1814-1880) was an influential English writer, best known for his adventure novels targeted at young readers. His works, particularly those with nautical themes, have captivated audiences with tales of heroism, exploration, and moral integrity. Debut: Kingston's literary journey began with the publication of The Circassian Chief in 1844. Genre: He specialized in seafaring adventure stories that were highly popular in the Victorian era. Output: Prolific in his writing, Kingston authored over 130 books, many focusing on nautical adventures and aimed at young readers. "Peter the Whaler"(1851): One of Kingston's early successes, detailing the adventures of a young whaler.

"The Three Midshipmen"(1873): Part of a series chronicling the exploits of British naval officers.

"The Three Admirals" (1891): Continuation of the naval adventure series, showcasing themes of bravery and exploration. Impact on Children's Literature: Kingston's adventure stories have had a lasting impact on children's literature, particularly in the adventure genre. Kingston's contributions to literature have made him a celebrated author, particularly known for his ability to inspire and entertain with stories of exploration and heroism. His works remain a testament to the adventurous spirit of the 19th century and continue to be enjoyed by readers around the world. Enduring Popularity: His tales of the high seas and distant lands continue to be appreciated for their timeless appeal and adventurous spirit. Kingston's contributions to literature have made him a celebrated author, particularly known for his ability to inspire and entertain with stories of exploration and heroism. His works remain a testament to the adventurous spirit of the 19th century and continue to be enjoyed by readers around the world.

CONTENTS

Chapter One

Sunshine Bill, according to the world's notion, was not "born with a silver spoon in his mouth;" but he had, which was far better, kind, honest parents. His mother kept an apple-stall at Portsmouth, and his father was part owner of a wherry; but even by their united efforts, in fine weather, they found it hard work to feed and clothe their numerous offspring.

Sometimes Sunshine Bill's father was laid up with illness, and sometimes his mother was so; and occasionally he and his brothers and sisters were sick also. Sometimes they had the measles, or small-pox, or a fever; and then there was the doctor to pay, and medicine to buy; consequently, at the end of these visitations, the family cash-box, consisting of an old stocking in a cracked basin, kept on the highest shelf of their sitting-room, was generally empty, and they considered themselves fortunate if they were not in debt besides. Still, no one ever heard them complain, or saw them quarrel, or beat their children, as some people do when things do not go straight with them; nor did their children ever fight among themselves. Even, indeed, in the worst of times, Sunshine Bill's mother managed to find a crust of bread and a bit of cheese, to keep the family from starving. To be sure, she and her husband could not give their children much of an education, as far as school learning was concerned. They themselves, in spite of all trials, were never cast down; and they taught Bill, and his brothers and sisters, to follow their example. They said that God had always been kind to them, and that they were sure He would not change while they tried to do their duty and please Him.

The most contented, and merriest, and happiest of their children was Sunshine Bill. That was not his real name, though; indeed, he did not get it till long after the time I am speaking of.

He was properly called William Sunnyside, for, curiously enough, Sunnyside was his father's name. His father was known as Merry Tom Sunnyside, and his mother as Pretty Molly Sunnyside—for pretty she had been when she was young, and good as she was pretty. It may seem surprising that they were not better off, but they began the world without anything, and children came fast upon them—a circumstance which keeps many people poor in worldly wealth.

Sunshine Bill, when still a very little fellow, found out how to keep the family pot boiling, even before some of his brothers had done so. No occupation came amiss to him. Sometimes he would go mud-larking, and seldom missed finding some treasure or other. The occupation was not a nice one, for the mud in Portsmouth Harbour is far from clean, or sweet to the nose; but Bill did not care for that, provided he was successful in his search. Sometimes, too, he would go fishing, and seldom came home without a pretty well-filled basket. Then he would look after seamen's boats, and place stools for passengers to walk along when the water was low; and when the weather was bad, and few persons were going afloat, he would go on errands, or scamper alongside gentlemen's horses, ready to hold them when they dismounted. He had such a merry, facetious manner about him, that he generally managed to pick up twice as much as anybody else engaged in the same sort of occupation.

This sort of work, however, was very well for Bill while he was a little fellow; but it was clear that it would not do for him when he should grow bigger. His father and mother often talked over what Bill was to do when that time came.

Tom Sunnyside wished to send him to sea after his two elder brothers, for his next two boys were with him in his boat. Molly wanted to keep him at home to help her in her trade; Bill was ready to do whatever they wished. He would serve his country afloat, and do his best to become an admiral, or he would sell apples all his life.

Nothing, however, was settled; and Bill continued to mud-lark, catch fish, run errands, look after boats, and hold gentlemen's horses, till he was getting to be a big lad.

At length a heavy affliction and trial overtook Mrs Sunnyside—Bill's mother. The wherry, with his father and two of his brothers, went off one November morning when it was blowing hard, with a passenger to a ship lying at Spithead. They put their fare all right on board, received payment, and shoved off from the ship. The gale increased, the weather thickened; hour after hour passed away, and the expected ones did not return to their home. Three days afterwards, a pilot vessel brought in an oar, and a board, with the rising sun painted on it.

The *Rising Sun* was the name of Tom Sunnyside's boat. Such was the only clue to his fate. Neither he, nor his boys, nor his boat, were ever seen again. The widow bowed her head, but she had no time to indulge in grief, for she had still several younger children to support.

She sat at her stall, and did her best to sell her apples. Bill exerted himself more than ever. His two elder brothers were, as has been said, on board men-of-war. The next two surviving children were girls, and could do little to help themselves or their mother. And now, for the first time, the family began to feel what it was to be hungry, and to have no food to put into their mouths. Bill was up early and late, and was always so hard at work that he declared he had no time to be hungry. The truth is, he might always have had plenty of food for himself, but that he thought fit to share every farthing of his gains among his brothers and sisters.

One day he was holding a horse for an officer, who was, he saw by his uniform, a commander in the navy, for Bill could distinguish the rank of naval officers by the gold lace on their coats, and knew at a glance a post captain from a commander, and a commander from a lieutenant, and so on. He especially liked the look of the officer whose horse he was holding; and while he walked it up and down as he had been directed, he thought to himself—

"If I was to go to sea now I should not only get a rig out, but have enough to eat, and be able to send home my pay to mother as soon as I get any."

He had just before been taking a survey of his clothes, which, in spite of all sorts of contrivances, he had no small difficulty in keeping about him. He wished to look tolerably decent, though he had considerable misgivings on that score. He felt very thin, and not so strong as he used to be, which is not surprising, considering the small amount of sustenance he took. The little ones at home were certainly fatter than he was.

When the officer came out of the house he cast a kind look at Bill, who, as was his custom to his superiors, pulled off his battered hat to him.

"I should like to know something about you, my lad," said the officer, as he mounted his horse, in a tone which was as kind as were his looks.

"Yes, sir," answered Bill, pulling a lock of his long, shaggy hair; "I be called Bill Sunnyside, and mother sells apples out at the corner of High Street, there."

"A succinct account of yourself, my lad," said the officer.

"It be true though, sir," said Bill, not understanding what succinct meant. "And, sir, I'd like to go to sea with you."

"Oh! Would you?" said the officer, smiling. "But how do you know that I command a ship?"

"Because you would not otherwise be in uniform," answered Bill, promptly.

"Ay, I see you have your wits about you," remarked the officer.

"It's as well I should, for they be the only things I have got except these duds," answered Bill, giving way to a propensity for humour, which, unknown to himself, he possessed, though he spoke with perfect respect.

The officer laughed, and said—

"Where is your father, boy?"

"He and two brothers were drowned out at Spithead, last autumn," answered Bill.

"Ah! I will have a talk with your mother, one of these days; I think I know her. Be a good boy meantime," said the officer, and he rode away up the street.

Bill looked after him, thinking when "one of these days" would come, and what would come out of the talk.

Several days passed by, and Bill heard nothing of the captain. His clothes became more and more tattered, and, though his mother mended them at night, they were so rotten that they often got torn again the next day. Winter came. Times were indeed hard with him. He grew thinner and thinner. Still, whenever he got a penny, he shared it with those he loved at home. "Never say die," was his motto; "it is a long lane which has no turning," and "a dull day when the sun does not shine out before the evening." With such expressions he used to cheer and comfort his mother, though, in spite of all trials, she was not often disposed to be more cast down than he was.

"Don't give way, mother," Bill used to say, when, on coming home in the evening, she looked sadder than usual. "Just remember what the parson said: 'The sun is shining up above the clouds every day in the year, and he is sure to break through them and shine upon us some time or other; and God is looking down at all times through them, let them be ever so thick, and never forgets us.'"

Still Bill could not help wishing that the kind captain had remembered, as he said he would, and made that some day or other arrive rather more quickly than there appeared a likelihood of its doing.

Chapter Two

There was not, I repeat, a more cheery, kind-hearted little woman in all Portsmouth, in spite of her large family, in spite of the loss of her husband, in spite of her poverty, than was Mrs Sunnyside; and this was just because God had given her a kind, happy heart, and she trusted in God, and knew that He loved her, and would not fail in any one of His promises. Had she not done that, she would soon have broken down.

"Well, Mrs Sunnyside, and how goes the world with you; and how is Bill?" said a gentleman, one day, coming up to the stall, where she sat knitting assiduously.

"Bill is at work, as he always is, and God has given health to those of my children who are spared, sir," said the widow, continuing her knitting, and only just glancing up at the gentleman's face. She then added, "I beg your pardon, sir, maybe I ought to know you, but you will excuse me when I say I don't."

"Very likely not," answered the gentleman, "yet I rather think I was a frequent customer of yours in former days, when I wore a midshipman's uniform. My business, however, is with your son Bill. He is my acquaintance. Tell me, Mrs Sunnyside, would you wish your boy to go to sea on board a man-of-war, with a captain who would keep an eye upon him, and give him a helping hand, if he proved himself worthy of it?"

Mrs Sunnyside did not answer at once. She went on knitting very slowly, though.

"Oh, sir! It would be a sore trial to part from Bill. He is the bright, cheering light of our little home. Yet the lad is fit for more than he is now doing; and I would be thankful, very thankful, if I thought he was with a kind, just captain, who would do as you say; but I would rather let Bill answer for himself."

"Well, Mrs Sunnyside, the truth is, I have asked Bill, and he told me that he should like to go to sea. He thinks he can help you better than by remaining at home. I must not, however, praise myself too much. I am

Captain Trevelyan. I command the *Lilly* sloop-of-war; and if Bill still wishes, as he did the other day, to go to sea, I will take him, and honestly look after him, and forward his true interests as far as justice to others will allow."

"Thank you, sir, thank you!" exclaimed Mrs Sunnyside. "If Bill wants to go, I will not say him nay; for I am sure you will do what you say, and a mother's prayers will be offered up for you and him every morning and night of my life. You see, sir, when I sit out here, I can often be thinking of you; and if anything does happen to you or Bill, I am sure it won't be for want of praying, nor for want of God's love; but just because He sees it's best."

"Have you taught Bill to hold these sentiments?" asked the gentleman.

"Well, sir, I know he thinks and does just as I think and do."

"Then, Mrs Sunnyside, I shall be very glad to have him with me. He will be one on whom I can depend on a pinch, and I shall like to think, when I am far away, that you are remembering me and him in your prayers, while you sit out here selling your apples. And here, Mrs Sunnyside, Bill's outfit, I know, is not very first-rate; take these three guineas, and spend them as you think best. You know as well as I do what he wants. And here is ten shillings in addition, just to put a little lining into Bill's and his brothers' and sisters' insides. A good meal or two will cheer you all up, and make things look brighter when Bill is going away. No thanks now; we understand each other, Mrs Sunnyside. When Bill is ready, he can come on board the *Lilly*— to-morrow, or next day; and ask for Mr Barker, the first lieutenant, to whom he can present this card. Now good-bye, Mrs Sunnyside, and I hope, when the ship is paid off three or four years hence, you will see Bill grown into a fine, big, strapping young seaman."

Saying this, Captain Trevelyan hurried away down the street.

"God bless you, sir! God bless you!" exclaimed Mrs Sunnyside, almost bursting into tears, for her feelings of gratitude overcame her.

That afternoon she had a wonderfully brisk sale for her apples, and was able to leave her post at an earlier hour than usual. She almost ran, in her eagerness to get home. Bill was out, but she hurried forth again to a slop-shop with which she was well acquainted. The shopmaster knew her. She felt sure he would treat her fairly, when she told him the state of the case. She knew Bill's height and width to the eighth of an inch. The great object was to get the things big enough. With a big bundle under her arm, she trudged home again, full of joy one moment at the thoughts of how happy his good luck would make him, and then ready to cry when she remembered that he would have to go away from her, and that for three, perhaps four years, or even more, she might not again see his bright, ruddy, smiling face; for, somehow or other, it was ruddy even when he was hungry.

"Who are all those things for, mother?" exclaimed Bill, with a look of surprise, as he came into the room and saw them hung up on the chairs and foot of the bed.

Mrs Sunnyside told him. At first, he could not speak. He used to long very much to go to sea; but now the reality had come suddenly upon him. When his brothers and sisters came in, they insisted on his putting on his new clothes. The bustle and talking revived him somewhat.

"I must go and have a wash first. I am not fit for these things," he answered, looking at his dirty clothes and hands; and out he rushed to the pump in the back yard, where he was wont to perform his ablutions. He returned for a piece of soap, however.

"I am going to do it right well," he said, "while I am about it."

He came back in about ten minutes, looking thoroughly fresh and clean. In the meantime, his mother and sister had laid the table for supper. It was not a very grand one, but more than usually abundant. There were hot sausages and toast, and maybe butter, or what did duty for butter, for it was very, very white, and tea, and some milk in a cream-jug.

"Well, I do feel as if I had been and done it right well!" exclaimed Bill, as he stood in a blue check shirt which his mother had sent out to him to put on after he had washed.

"Now, Bill, do try this on," she said, handing him a pair of trousers. They fitted nicely round the waist; no braces were needed. Then she made him put his arms into the jacket, and fasten a black silk handkerchief round his neck with a sailor's knot. And then his sister came behind, and clapped on a broad-brimmed, low-crowned hat, with a long ribbon round it, hanging down on one side.

"There! There! How well he does look!"

"Bill, you do, darling!" exclaimed his mother. "Every inch a sailor. Bless you, Bill!" His brothers and sisters made some of these remarks, and many others; and came round, taking him by the hand, or patting him on the back, and Bill stood by smiling and well pleased. He had never in his life been so nicely dressed. Then they brought him a pair of low shoes. He thought them rather incumbrances, but he put them on for the honour of the thing; and they had broad ribbon bows in front, and did look very natty, to be sure.

In their eagerness they almost forgot the sausages, which were somewhat overdone—burnt all on one side; but that did not matter much, and at length they all sat down, and while they were laughing and talking, the sausages hissed and spluttered in return, as much as to say, "We are all ready; we wish you would eat us. You look so merry and happy, and perhaps we shall be merry and happy too."

Bill at first could not eat much for thinking that at last he was going on board a man-of-war. No more could his mother, but when the rest began to eat away, he followed their example; and his mother at last managed to get down the remaining sausage, which all her children insisted she should have, Susan giving it a fresh heating up before the fire, for they had a good fire that day. Many a winter's evening they had had to go without it, for want of something to burn. At last there was not as much left as a piece of grease in the dish, nor a piece of bread on the platter, and all the tea was drained to the last drop; and then Bill stood up and thanked God for their good supper.

"And it was a good one!" cried out little Tommy. "A right good one. And, Bill, I hope you may get many such aboard ship."

"Maybe," said Bill, "but they will not be like this, for there will be none of you there; and after all it's not the grub, but it's them that eats it with us that makes it pleasant."

Bill might have said more but he did not; for a good reason—he could not just then trust his voice; so he jumped up and began to dance a hornpipe, though he was not very perfect in the art of dancing.

"Never mind," he said, "I will learn something more about that too, when I get to sea."

Bill was up betimes, dressed in his new suit. "Mother, I would like to carry your basket for you," he said. "Maybe it's the last day I shall be able to do it."

"No, no, Bill," she said; "I am not going out this morning, till you are away. We will go down to the Point, and learn when the *Lilly* is going out of harbour. It is better to go on board now than to wait till she gets out to Spithead."

It was a hard matter for Bill to wish all his brothers and sisters good-bye, and harder still to part from his mother, but he did it in a brave, hearty way. Old Joe Simmons, who had known him all his life, and known his mother too, for that matter, since she was born, insisted on taking him off.

"The *Lilly* will be going out of harbour to-day, or to-morrow at farthest, and the sooner you are aboard, my boy, the better," said old Joe, taking Bill's bundle from Mrs Sunnyside. "Come along with me. And now, Mrs Sunnyside, do you go back, there's a good woman, now. I'll look after your boy, and see him all right aboard. I know three or four of her crew who shipped from here, and I will speak to one or two of them, and they will put Bill up to what he ought to do, so that he won't seem like a green-horn when they get to sea. There's the captain of the maintop, Jack Windy, son of an old shipmate of mine, and he will stand Bill's friend, if I ask him. And there's little Tommy Rebow, who has been to sea for a year or more; and I'll just tell him I will break every bone in his body if he don't behave right to Bill. So, you see, he will have no lack of friends, Mrs Sunnyside. There now, good-bye, good-bye! Bless you, missus! Bless you! Don't fret, now; Bill will be all right."

These words the old man uttered, as he pushed his wherry from the beach, and pulled up the harbour towards a fine corvette which lay at anchor off Gosport.

Chapter Three

The *Lilly* was a fine, rakish-looking corvette, with a crew of one hundred and twenty, officers and seamen, as Joe Simmons informed Bill.

The old man went up the side with him.

"There's the first lieutenant," he said. "You just go up and tell him you have come aboard. It will be all right. Although he looks very grand, he is all right at bottom; and I have heard more than one thing in his favour. He won't eat you; so don't be afear'd, Bill."

Bill did as he was advised, and presented the captain's card. Mr Barker glanced at it.

"Oh! You are Bill Sunnyside. We will enter you. Master-at-arms, see to this boy."

"It's all right, boy, you can go forward!"

Bill, thus dismissed, gladly rejoined his old friend, thankful that the dreaded interview was over. He would not have minded it if the captain had been aboard, for he had taken a great fancy to him, and felt ready to go through fire and water to serve him.

Old Joe introduced him, as he had promised, to a fine, active-looking seaman who had just come from aloft, with hands well tarred, and a big clasp knife hung by a rope round his neck. Jack Windy was every inch a sailor.

"Oh, ay, Joe! No fear; we'll look after the lad," he said, giving an approving glance at Bill. "We will make a prime seaman of him, never you fear. And here, Tommy Rebow, you just come here, boy. You show Bill here what he will have to do, and what he must not do; and none of your jackanape tricks—mind that."

Thus Bill had not been many minutes on board before he found himself with several acquaintances. Old Joe, satisfied that all was right, wished him good-bye.

"There, Bill," he said, taking him by the hand, "just do you go on doing what you have been, and there's One who will look after you, and knows better how to do so than I could, or your own father, if he was alive, or the captain himself; and when I say my prayers—and I do say them, and so must you, Bill—I will put in a word about you; and I am sure your mother will, and your brothers and sisters as is big enough; and you see, Bill, you have every reason to go away contented and happy. Now good-bye, lad, God bless you!"

And again old Joe wrung Sunshine Bill's hand, and went down the side of the ship into his wherry.

"Now, do you mind, Bill," he shouted, as, taking his seat, he seized the sculls and sprung them briskly into the water. Once more he stopped, and, resting his oars for a moment, waved another farewell with his right hand.

The men had just been piped to breakfast when Bill went on board, and the ship was comparatively quiet. In a short time, however, all was bustle and seeming confusion. The officers were shouting, the boatswain was piping, and the men hurrying here and there along the decks or up the rigging; some bending sails, others hoisting in stores, or coming off, or going away in boats. Bill had often been on board ship, so it was not so strange to him as it would have been to many boys. Yet he had never before formed one of a ship's company, and he could not help feeling that he might at any moment be called upon to perform some duty or other with which he was totally unacquainted.

"Never you fear, Bill," said Tommy Rebow, who observed his anxiety. "I will put you up to anything you want to know. Just you stick by me."

Presently a quartermaster ordered Tommy to lay hold of a rope and haul away; and Bill ran and helped him, and quickly got the rope taut, when an officer sung out, "Belay," and Tommy made the rope fast. This was the first duty Bill ever performed in the service of his country.

After this, whenever there was any pulling or hauling, Bill ran and helped, unless ordered elsewhere. Though he could not always remember the names of the ropes, still he felt that he was making himself useful.

Amidst the bustle, he at length heard the first lieutenant sing out, "Man the sides." The boatswain's whistle sounded. The sideboys stood with the white man-ropes in their hands, the officers collected on either side of the gangway. The marines hurried from below with their muskets, and stood, drawn up in martial array; and presently Bill saw a boat come alongside, and an officer in full uniform, whom he at once recognised as Captain Trevelyan, stepped upon deck. Saluting the officers by lifting his hat, he spoke a few kind, good-natured words to them, and then gave a scrutinising glance along the decks, turning his eyes aloft.

"You have made good progress, Mr Barker. I hope we shall go out to Spithead to-morrow," he observed. "How many hands do you still want?" he asked.

"We have our complement complete, sir," was the answer.

"Has that boy I spoke to you about come on board—Sunnyside?"

"Yes, sir; he came on board this morning. He is a sharp lad, and will make a good seaman."

Bill would have been proud, had he known that he was the subject of conversation between the captain and first lieutenant.

The next morning the *Lilly* cast off from the buoy to which she was moored, and, making sail, ran out to Spithead, where she again anchored. Bill thought he should now be fairly off to sea, but she had another week to remain there. There was the powder to take on board, and more provisions; then there were despatches from the Admiralty. At length Blue Peter was hoisted. All boats were ordered away from the ship's side. Once more sail was made, and with the wind from the north-east the *Lilly* glided down the calm waters of the Solent.

Bill was soon perfectly at home among his new shipmates. He had never been so well fed in his life—plenty of good boiled beef and potatoes, and sweet biscuit.

"I have often wished to come to sea, and I am very glad I have come," he said, as he was seated at mess. "I did not think they fed us so well."

"Just you wait till we have been a few months in blue water, youngster," observed Sam Grimshaw—"old Grim," as his shipmates called him—"when we get down to the salted cow and pickled horse, and pork which is all gristle and bone. You will then sing a different tune, I have a notion."

Old Grim was noted for grumbling. He grumbled at everything; and as to pleasing him, that was out of the question.

"Well," answered Bill, "all I can say is, I am thankful for the good things now I've got them; and when the bad come, it will be time enough to cry out. I used to think, too, when once a ship got into the Channel clear away from the land, there would be nothing but tumbling and tossing about; and here we are running on as smoothly as we might up Portsmouth Harbour. Now, I am thankful for that."

"Well, so it's as well to be, my lad, for before many days are over we may be tumbling about in a heavy gale under close-reefed topsails, and then you will sing another tune to what you are doing now."

"I shall be singing that I know the bad weather won't last for ever, and that I have no doubt the sun will shine out," answered Bill.

"But maybe you will get washed overboard, or a loose block will give you a knock on the head and finish you, or some other mishap will befall you," growled out old Grim.

"As to that," answered Bill, "I am ready for the rough and smooth of life, and for the ups and downs. As I hope to have some of the ups, I must make up my mind to be content with a few of the downs."

"Well, well! There's no making you unhappy," growled out old Grim. "Now, you don't mean to say this duff is fit food for Christians," he exclaimed, sticking his fork into a somewhat hard piece of pudding.

"It's fit for hungry boys at sea," answered Bill; "and I only wish that my brothers and sisters had as good beef and pork for dinner, not to speak of peas-pudding and duff, as we have got every day. I should like to send them some of mine, and yours too, if you do not eat it."

"Well, as we cannot live on nothing, I am obliged to eat it, good or bad," answered old Grim; "and as to giving you some of mine, why, I don't see that there's overmuch I get for myself."

"I did not ask it for myself, and I am glad to see you do not find it too bad to eat after all," said Bill, observing that old Grim cleared his plate of every particle of food it contained.

Tommy Rebow used to amuse himself by trying to tease Grimshaw, not that he would stand much from him, or from anybody else; and often Tommy had to make a quick jump of it to get out of his way. Still he would return to the charge till Grim got fearfully vexed with him. Bill himself never teased old Grim or anybody else. It was not his nature. He could laugh with them as much as they might please, but he never could laugh at them, or jeer them. Old Grim really liked Bill, though he took an odd way of showing it sometimes. Bill, indeed, soon became a favourite on board, just because he was so good-natured and happy, and was ready to oblige any one.

Captain Trevelyan did not forget his promise to Bill's mother; and though of course he did not say much to the lad, it was very evident that he had his eye on him, as he had indeed, more or less, on everybody on board. He took care that Bill should learn his duties. There were several young gentlemen on board in the midshipman's berth; and the captain had for their use a model built of the ship's masts and rigging. He used to have them up every morning in fine weather, and make them learn all the names and uses of the ropes. Then he would make them put the ship about, or wear ship, or heave her to. Then he would have the yards braced up, then squared, then braced up on the other tack, and so forth. The ship's boys were made to stand by, to watch these proceedings, and then they were called up to go through the manoeuvres themselves, the boatswain, or one of the masters, giving them lessons. Bill was very quick in learning, and so, before they got half way across the Atlantic, he knew how to put the ship about almost as well as any body on board. He soon, indeed, caught Tommy Rebow up, and as they were both well-grown lads, they were placed in the mizzen-top. Both of them soon learned to lay out on the yards, and to reef and furl the mizzen-topsail as well as anybody.

"Come, Bill, I told Joe Simmons I would learn you all I know myself," said Jack Windy, "and now you are getting seamanship, it's time you should be learning the hornpipe. You have a good ear, because you can sing well, as I have heard you; so you should learn to dance it, to astonish the natives wherever we go."

Captain Trevelyan had secured a fiddler among his ship's company—a negro of jet black hue, with a face all crumpled up in a most curious fashion, with great white rolling eyeballs, and huge thick lips. He was not a beauty, and he did not think so himself; but he prided himself on playing the fiddle, and well, too, he did play it. His name was Diogenes Snow; but he was called Dio, or Di sometimes, for shortness. With his music, and under Jack Windy's instruction, Bill soon learned to dance a hornpipe, so that few could surpass him.

"Dare, Bill; well done, Bill!" shouted Dio, as he scraped away with might and main. "Oh, golly! Iolly! Bill would beat Queen Charlotte, if she tried to do it, dat he would. Berry well, Bill. Keep moving, boy! Dat's it! One more turn! Hurrah! Hurrah!"

Chapter Four

The *Lilly* had been ordered to proceed direct to Jamaica. She was already in the latitude of the West Indies, and might expect to get into Port Royal in the course of six or eight days. Hitherto the weather had been remarkably fine, though the wind had been generally light. There was now, however, a dead calm. The dog-vanes hung up and down, the sails every now and then giving sullen flaps against the masts, while the ship rolled slowly—so slowly as scarcely to allow the movement to be perceptible—from side to side. The ocean was as smooth as the smoothest mirror, not a ripple, not the slightest cat's-paw being perceptible on it. Instead, however, of its usual green colour, it had become of a dead leaden hue, the whole arch of heaven being also spread with a dark grey canopy of a muddy tint. Yet, though the sun was not seen, the heat, as the day drew on, became intense. Dio was the only person on board who did not seem to feel it, but went about his duties as cook's mate with as much zeal and alacrity as ever, scrubbing away at pots and pans, scraping potatoes, and singing snatches of odd nigger songs. His monkey Queerface, brought from his last ship, just paid off on her return from the West Indies, was skipping about the fore-rigging, now hanging by his tail swinging to and fro, now descending with the purpose of attempting to carry off one of the boy's hats, then failing, scudding hand over hand up the rigging again like lightning, chattering and spluttering as he watched the rope's end lifted threateningly towards him, or dodging the bit of biscuit or rotten potato thrown at his head. The watch on deck were hanging listlessly about, finding even their usual employment irksome. A few old hands might have been seen making a grummit or pointing a rope, while the sailmaker and his crew were at work on a suite of boat-sails; here and there also a marine might have been seen cleaning his musket, but finding the barrel rather hotter to touch than was pleasant. In truth, everywhere it was hot: below, hotter still. Though the sun was not shining, there was no shade; and discontented spirits kept moving about, in vain trying to find a cooler spot than the one they had left. Old Grim did nothing but growl.

"If it's hot out here, what will it be when we gets ashore?" he growled out. "Why, we shall be regularly roasted or baked, and the cannibals won't have any trouble in cooking us. But to my mind (and I have always said it) a sailor is the most unfortunate chap alive, one day dried up in these burning latitudes, and then sent to cool his nose up among the icebergs. It's all very well for Dio there. It's his nature to like heat. For us poor white-skinned chaps, it's nothing but downright cruelty."

"But I suppose that it won't be always like this," said Bill. "We shall have the sun shine, and a breeze, one of these days, and go along merrily through the water. There's no place, that I ever heard tell of, where the sun does not shine, and though we don't see him, he is shining as bright as ever up above the clouds, even now. He has only got to open a way for himself through them, and we shall soon see him again."

"As to the sun shining always, you are wrong there, young chap," growled out old Grim. "Up at the North Pole there, there's a night of I don't know how many months, when you don't see him at all."

"You are wrong there, Grim," cried out Jack Windy. "I once shipped aboard a whaler, and we were shut up all the winter in the ice, and during the time we every day caught a sight of the red head of the old sun, just popping up above the horizon to the southward, and a comfort that was, I can tell you, particularly when we saw him getting higher and higher, and knew that summer was coming back again, and that we should have the ice breaking away, and get set free once more."

"Yes, yes!" exclaimed Bill, exultingly, "I am sure the sun shines everywhere, and though you might have got a long night in winter, you got a longer day in summer, I'll warrant."

"You are right there, boy," said Jack Windy. "For days together, in the north there, the sun never sets, and so, as you say, we have a very long day."

"I thought so!" exclaimed Bill, quite delighted. "Whatever else happens, God takes care to give us a right share of sunshine, and more than a right share too, if we reckon upon what we deserve."

A portion of the crew were below, but one after the other they came up, complaining that the between-decks was more like a stew-pan or hothouse than any place they had ever before been in. The officers also made their appearance on deck; but though they began to walk up and down as usual, one after the other they stopped and leant against the bulwarks or a gun-carriage, turning their faces round as if to catch a breath of air. The dog-vanes, however, hung down as listlessly as ever.

"Not an air in the heavens, sir," observed Mr Truck, the master, as Captain Trevelyan came on deck. "I cannot make anything of the weather."

"But I can," exclaimed the captain, taking a hurried glance to the westward. "What is that, do you think?"

He pointed to what seemed a long bank of driven snow rising out of the horizon. It extended nearly half-way round the horizon, every instant getting higher and higher.

"All hands shorten sail!" shouted the captain. "Up aloft, there! Lay out, haul down!"

The words produced a magical effect. In a minute, the listless crew were all activity and life. Up the rigging they swarmed like bees, some throwing themselves into the tops, others ascending the topgallant yards, and running out to either yard-arm, till every part of the ship swarmed with life, those on deck pulling and hauling with might and main, the officers assisting, every idler putting a hand to a rope. The topsails were quickly clewed up and furled, the other sails were handed, but scarcely were the men off the yards, than the high bank of foam approached the ship. There was a loud rushing, roaring noise.

"Down for your lives!" shouted the captain.

"Down for your lives, my lads," repeated the lieutenants; and though the helm was put up, and the fore-topmast staysail hoisted, the wind, striking the tall ship, drove her down before it. Over she heeled. Down, down she went. It seemed as if she was never to rise again. The bravest held their breath. Many a cheek turned pale with fear. The captain waved his hand to the carpenter and his mates.

"Axes!" he shouted. They knew what that meant.

"I knew it would be so," growled old Grim who was standing near Bill, holding on to the weather bulwarks. "First a calm, to dry the sap out of a fellow's bones, and then a gale, to blow his teeth down his throat."

"But there may be a calm again or a fair breeze, and the sun will shine out bright and clear," answered Bill, who, however, felt more inclined to think that his last day had come, than he had ever been before. As he looked out, there was the sea, hitherto so smooth, now leaping and raging, and covered with seething foam, the spoon-drift flying in vast sheets of white, from top to top of its broken summits, while huge watery mountains seemed about to burst over the deck. Still, he knew very well that sailors had to expect rough seas as well as smooth, and that many a ship had been in a worse predicament and had escaped. As the captain cried out "axes," the carpenter and his men sprang aft, with their shining weapons in their hands. Just then the ship gave a bound, it seemed like a race-horse darting forward. Up she rose, her head springing round, and feeling the power of the helm, away she flew before the hurricane.

"Square away the fore-yards!" shouted the captain (the after-yards had already been squared). The ship's company saw that the immediate danger was passed, and once more, fore and aft, all hands breathed freely.

"The sun will soon be shining out!" exclaimed Bill cheerily, within old Grim's hearing.

"Don't be too sure of that, boy," growled out the latter. "We shall be broaching to, maybe, before long, and be in a worse case than we were just now. I have heard of a ship doing that, running under bare poles, and getting every soul of her crew washed off her deck, except three—the black cook, the caulker's mate, and the captain's steward—and a pretty job they had to find their way into port, seeing that neither of them knew anything of navigation, or seamanship either, for that matter; and I should like to know whose case you would be in, Sunshine Bill, if you were left with Dio and Ned Farring, aboard this craft?"

"All I can say is, I hope we should do our best, and trust to Providence," answered Bill. "I have never heard that a man can do more than that, and that's what I hope I shall always do, as long as I have life."

On went the *Lilly* before the still increasing hurricane. The topgallant masts were struck, and topmasts housed, the yards secured by rolling tackles, and the ship made as snug as she could be. This was done not a bit too soon, for it was evident that she was about to encounter one of the fiercest of West Indian hurricanes, such as have sent many a stout ship to the bottom.

Chapter Five

The wind howled, and shrieked, and whistled in the rigging, the seas roared and dashed against the sides of the corvette, as under bare poles she rushed on amidst them. Now she rose to the summit of a dark green mountainous billow, with its crest all leaping, foaming, and hissing; then she glided rapidly down its side, as if it had been an ice-mountain, into the dark valley below, again to rise up more slowly to the top of another sea, suddenly to find herself once more in the deep trough, with a huge curling wave reaching almost to her tops, threatening to break over her. Two of the quartermasters were at the helm. The officers were all on deck, the crew at their stations. No one could tell what might next happen.

"If the wind holds as it does now, we shall be all right," observed Mr Truck, the master, "but if it shifts, we may find ourselves running in among some ugly navigation, and our best chance is to scud as we are doing."

"Hurricanes always do shift," observed Captain Trevelyan: "but we must hope for the best. The wind may hold in its present quarter for some time to come."

"Well, Bill, what do you think of this here breeze?" asked Tommy Rebow. "I was telling you it blew pretty stiffish out in these parts."

"Why, that if I had my choice, I would rather it did not blow so hard; but then do you see, Tommy, we have not got our choice, and it's for us to take the weather as we find it. I am very sure that God has got His reasons for sending this hurricane,—though maybe we don't see them,—and so it's our business to make the best of it."

"Maybe," put in old Grim; "but I have a notion you won't be so content as you are now, when it comes on to blow ten times harder. I tell you I am expecting every moment to see the ship come right up, with one of those seas breaking clean over her, and then there will be 'cut away the masts' in earnest, if there's time for it, and if not, we shall all go to the bottom together."

Jack Windy and two or three other men who heard old Grim growling out these remarks, burst into a loud laugh. "Why, any one would suppose you had taken a double dose of growling-powder, old Grim," exclaimed Jack. "Do you want to frighten these young chaps, or not? If you do, maybe they will be taking a turn out of you one of these days. Of course it may blow, and a good deal harder than it does now; but the *Lilly* is not a craft to mind a cap full of wind, more or less, and she will weather a worse gale than this, I have a notion."

Night was coming on. The hurricane raged as fiercely as ever; the light grew greyer and greyer, till, by degrees, a black darkness settled down over the ocean. Still the seas rose up more wild and fierce-looking every instant, and the ship rushed on, seemingly into space. Sharp eyes only could see beyond the jib-boom, yet there were some who could have pierced even that thick darkness, if there had been anything to see besides the tossing seas. They, however, only appeared leaping up ahead and round the ship, as if each one was eager to get hold of her, and carry her down to the depths of old ocean. On, on she flew. The captain and master frequently cast anxious looks at the compass in the binnacle, while the second lieutenant with the boatswain went forward and stood on the forecastle, peering with all their might and main into the darkness ahead. Not a few other eyes were trying to look out ahead also; but it seemed as if all the eyes and all the looking would do little to discover any object, till the ship was too close to avoid it. The seconds appeared like minutes, the minutes hours, as thus the corvette rushed on. Not a man spoke. In truth, speaking, except at the top of the voice, was of little use, the howling of the wind and the roaring of the sea drowning all other sounds.

At length, however, there came a cry from forward, such as a seaman alone could give. "Breakers! Breakers! On the starboard bow!" It reached right aft, sounding high above the hurricane.

"Starboard the helm!" cried the captain.

There were few on board who did not hold their breath, till they were obliged to gasp for more. It seemed as if the last moments of the ship and all on board were approaching. Yet there was no sign of terror; not a man quitted his station. The captain sprang into the starboard rigging and looked anxiously out on that side. His eye distinguished breakers, and his ear the increased roaring of the seas, as they dashed against the rocky impediment to their course. Would the ship weather the reef, and if she did, were there more reefs ahead? On she flew; but the compass showed that she had come up a little to the wind: still there was now the danger, as her bows met the seas, of their breaking on board.

"Hold on! Hold on for your lives!" shouted the second lieutenant, as he and the boatswain, clinging desperately to the fore-stay, saw a huge sea about to break over the ship's bows. On it came. It was upon them, and over them it burst, deluging the deck, and almost tearing them from their hold. The crew clung to whatever they could grasp. On rolled the sea across the deck, with difficulty finding its way through the scuppers, the greater bulk at length breaking open a port, and thus getting free, a considerable quantity of water, however, finding its way down below.

"If another sea like that comes aboard us, we shall be sent to the bottom!" exclaimed old Grim, shaking himself from the water, which had covered him from head to foot. "It's lucky you boys have got paws to hold on by, like Master Queerface there, or you would have broken biscuit for the last time."

Neither Bill nor Tommy made any answer. Tommy, in fact, was more frightened than he had ever before been in his life, and Bill could not help feeling that the ship was in no small danger. Still he thought to himself,— "There's One looking after us who can help us better than we can ourselves, and so why should I cry out till I have got something to cry for?"

Many on board who saw the breakers, expected every instant to hear the fearful crash of the ship driving on the pointed rocks, to see the masts falling, and the seas come leaping triumphantly over the shattered wreck; but it was not to be so.

The first danger was passed, and no other sign of breakers was perceived. The master had gone below to examine the chart.

"We may keep her before the wind again," he said. "All is clear ahead, for if any of those ugly seas were to break on board, it might play havoc with the barky."

The longest night has an end. In the middle of the watch, the hurricane began to abate, and though the seas tumbled and rolled, and leaped and roared, with almost unabated fury, it was evident that there was much less wind. At length the fore-topsail was set, closely reefed, and the ship ran bounding on from sea to sea, as if escaping from the huge billows which came roaring up astern. Next the foresail was set. Another sail succeeded, till once more, under her usual sail, in spite of the heavy sea still running, the ship was hauled up on her course, a long way out of which she had for some time been running. The sun shone forth, casting his beams on the white crests of the seas, making them glitter and shine like frosted silver.

"Well, Grimshaw," said Bill, addressing old Grim, "the sun has come out, as I said he would, and the hurricane has had its blow, and we shall have fine weather again presently."

"Don't you be boasting too much about that, youngster," answered old Grim. "You don't know what is going to happen next, and you will be laughing on the wrong side of your mouth before long, so look out for squalls, boy."

No one minded what old Grim said, so these remarks made but little impression on Bill, and he went about his duties with as much briskness as ever. Bill was a favourite on board; no doubt about that, both among officers and men. The lieutenants had applied to have him appointed as one of the boys in the gun-room. It would give him more work; but Bill was ready for that at all times.

The sun had set. It was rapidly growing dark, when the watch on deck were ordered to take a reef out of each of the topsails. Bill and Tommy Rebow sprang up the mizen rigging, as they were both in the mizen-top, and were soon lying out on the mizen-topsail yard. They were both in high spirits, feeling up to anything at the moment. One of the older topmen was in the lee-earing. Bill was next to him. Tommy came next. Suddenly the ship gave a tremendous lurch. There was a cry.

"Where's Bill?" exclaimed Tommy, a horror coming over his heart.

"A man overboard! A man overboard!" was shouted from the mizen-top. It was echoed from below.

At that instant the captain came on deck. In falling, Bill had struck the chain-span of the weather-quarter davits, breaking it as if it had been packthread. Mr Collinson, the second lieutenant, who had charge of the deck, pointed it out to the captain.

"The poor fellow must have been killed, whoever he was."

"Who is it?" asked the captain.

"Sunshine Bill!" cried out a voice.

"Bill Sunnyside, sir," said another.

"Alas!" thought the captain, "the poor lad I promised his widowed mother I would look after. Does any one see him?" asked the captain.

"Yes, sir; there he is! There he is!" answered several voices.

Bill was seen floating on the top of a foaming sea. The life-buoy was let go, its bright light bursting forth, and burning a welcome beacon, it might be, to poor Bill. He was known to be a good swimmer. No boy was equal to him on board. The ship was flying away, however, at a rapid rate from him. Many declared that they saw him swimming, and that therefore he could not have been killed, as had been supposed. Captain Trevelyan gazed for an instant at the spot where Bill had been seen. He was no longer, however, visible. It was a moment to him of intense anxiety. To lower a boat in that foaming sea would in all probability cause the loss of many more, and yet could he desert the poor lad?

Suddenly, with startling energy, he shouted out, "Wear ship! Up with the helm! Square away the after-yards!"

The ship went on plunging into the heavy seas as she made a wide circuit, the yards being again braced up on the other tack.

Chapter Six

The *Lilly*, brought to the wind, once more stood back along the course on which she had just before been sailing. She was then hove to. By the captain's calculations, she had reached the locality where Bill had fallen overboard. All hands were on deck and every eye strained, endeavouring to pierce the thick gathering gloom in the direction where it was supposed he might still be.

Friendly voices shouted out, — "Bill Sunnyside! Sunshine Bill! Answer, lad! Answer!" Still no reply came.

"I knew it would be so," muttered old Grim. "The lad was always boasting of being in such good luck, or something of that sort. And now this is what his good luck has come to. Well, well, his fate has been that of many, so there's nothing strange in it."

With this philosophical remark old Grim walked forward; but still, somehow or other, his heart felt sorry at losing the poor lad, and he went and peered down to leeward and then looked to windward again, in the hopes that his eyes, which were among the sharpest on board, might catch a glimpse of the lad. If he was clinging to the life-buoy he might be all right, but where that was, was the question. Minutes passed away, and still no one could discover Bill. The captain pulled out his watch and went to the binnacle-lamp.

"Twenty minutes," he remarked to Mr Collinson. "A strong man could scarcely swim as long in such a sea as this."

"But he may have got hold of the buoy, sir," observed Mr Collinson.

"True! If he has, I wish we could see him. I do not like to give him up."

Another five minutes passed. Again the captain looked at his watch. The time had appeared an age to him, as it had to most on board. He took another turn on deck, and then looked out once more.

"Does nobody see him?" he asked; and there was sorrow and regret in his tone.

There was no answer. The silence was very sad. Once more he returned to the lamp.

"Half an hour has passed," he observed to Mr Barker. "I am afraid the matter is hopeless."

"I am afraid so too," answered the lieutenant, who was a kind-hearted man.

"It must be done!" he said. "Hands, wear ship!" he shouted out, in a startling voice, evidently giving the order with no good will.

The men were hurrying to their stations to obey it, when Grimshaw shouted out: —

"I heard a voice. It's Bill! It's Bill! Away to windward there!"

"Silence, fore and aft," cried the captain; and directly afterwards, borne down by the gale, there came a loud, strange, wild cry.

"That's him! There's no mistake about it," cried Grimshaw; "hurrah!"

The crew gave a shout in reply.

"It will keep up the poor fellow's spirits," observed the captain. "Now, silence, men." And now the awful thought crossed his mind, "Can I allow a boat to be lowered in this broken, heavy sea, with the greatest probability of her being capsized, and all hands in her lost?" These words were uttered partly aloud.

"I'll go in her, sir," said Mr Collinson. "There will be no lack of volunteers."

"Volunteers alone then must go," answered the captain. "The risk is a fearful one, yet I cannot allow the poor lad to perish."

Scarcely had Mr Collinson shouted out, "I am going, lads! Volunteers for the boat," than numbers of the crew came rushing aft, Jack Windy and Grimshaw among them.

"I don't suppose we shall pick up the lad, after all," growled the latter, "but we ought to try, I suppose."

As no man pulled a stouter oar than he did, Mr Collinson gladly accepted him, as he did Windy.

Four other men were selected, and waiting for a favourable lull, the boat was lowered. The bowman, however, in shoving off, lost his balance, and overboard he went. Happily, the man next to him had just time to seize him by the leg, and haul him in, though not without difficulty his oar was saved. Not without sad forebodings of the fate of the boat's crew, did the captain see her leave the ship's side.

"No man can handle a boat better than Collinson," he observed to Mr Barker, who was by his side, "that's one comfort."

Away the boat pulled amidst the foaming broken seas, and was soon lost to sight in the thick gloom which had settled down over the ocean.

"I should be thankful to see something of them again," observed the captain to Mr Barker. "The boat has been a long time away. How long do you think?"

"I did not look at my watch when she was lowered," answered the first lieutenant, "but it is some time; yet the sea is a dangerous one; but, as you say, sir, Collinson is wonderful handy in a boat, and he and his crew will do what men can do, there is no doubt about that."

Still the captain looked very anxious, so did others on board. Even in the attempt to pick up Bill, should he have floated so long, the boat might be swamped. It was the most critical time; for the helmsman looking towards the man he wished to save, might watch with less care the approach of a curling sea. Had old Grim been on board he would have been prognosticating dire disaster, but as he had gone away in the boat, he knew better than anybody else on board, what had happened. Many had become very anxious. Tommy Rebow, who was very fond of Bill, as well as of Jack Windy, wrung his hands, almost bursting into tears, as, not seeing them return, he began to fear that they both had been lost.

Meantime, where was Bill? On falling from aloft, and striking the chain-span, which, though it did not break his bones, broke his fall, he bounded off into the foaming sea. How he had not been killed he could not tell, but one thing was certain, it was not his head that struck the chain, but, as Jack Windy observed, it was the other end of his body. The fact at all events was, that he reached the foaming raging water not at all the worse for his fall. Though he went under for a moment, he soon rose with his head above the surface. He turned himself round once or twice to ascertain that all was right as far as his body was concerned, and then quietly contented himself with keeping his head as high above the foam as he well could. He did not think about sharks, or it might have made him still more uncomfortable. As to swimming after the ship, that he knew to be an impossibility.

"If I swim at all I shall only tire myself," he thought, so he just threw himself on his back, and kept his eyes fixed on the ship, as she flew away from him.

"It will be some time before she can be up to me again," he thought. "Captain Trevelyan is not the man to desert one of his people, even a little chap like me, and maybe he will remember what he said to my mother. If I keep my clothes on me, I shall not be able to float as long as without them."

Thinking thus, for he did not utter the words aloud, he managed to kick off one shoe, then the other. He felt lighter without them. The trousers were next to be got rid of. There was some risk in pulling them off, lest he might get his feet entangled in them, but a sailor's trousers are not very large. So Bill managed to draw up one of his legs and get hold of the foot of the trousers; then he slipped the other leg quickly out, and off went his trousers after his shoes. His shirt was the next thing to be rid of, but there was a risk of the tails getting over his head, so he rolled them up, and then getting one arm clear, in a twinkling whisked it off, and there he was, floating out in the ocean, with no more clothes on than when he was born; but he felt much lighter, and when the seas came roaring round him he kept his head more easily out of the curling foam. While getting off his clothes, he saw the life-buoy, with its bright light bursting forth, drop into the water, but it was too far off for him to attempt to reach it in that troubled sea. Though, as has been said, he knew his captain too well to dread that he would desert him, it was a sore trial of his faith to see the ship sail on and on, till she vanished into gloom. He had seen the ship wore round several times on different occasions. He knew that was the way of getting her head in another direction, in such a sea as was now running.

"The captain will not leave me; no, no fear of that," he thought, and presently, once more, as if to reward his confidence, he saw the ship appearing again through the gloom. On she came, nearer and nearer. He longed to strike out towards her, but he felt that the attempt would be useless, so he still lay floating with his hands moving, to prevent being rolled over and over by the seas. On she came, her dark masts and sails seen clearly against the sky, but she seemed about to pass him at a distance. Then he saw her heave-to. And now his heart beat anxiously. Would a boat be sent to pick him up? He was still too far away to give him a hope of reaching it by swimming. He thought, too, — "If I sing out I shall exhaust myself, and be unable to keep afloat;" so he lay as before, hoping only as a person in his position could hope, that a boat might be lowered. Yet he had been long enough at sea to know the danger of the operation. He had heard of boats being lowered in such a sea as was then running, and all hands being lost out of them. He waited and waited. It seemed to him not as if one hour, but hour after hour passed away, and there lay the ship, and yet no one on board could see him, nor could he make himself heard, as he thought.

"They are looking for me, there's no doubt about that," he said to himself; "but I wish they would send a boat."

If the water had been cold he could not have kept up, but it was just pleasant, and he felt his strength in no way exhausted. At length, amid the hurly-burly and clashing of the sea round him, although the corvette was a long way to leeward, he heard Captain Trevelyan's voice shouting out, "Up with the helm! Square away the after-yards!"

"Now," thought Bill, "I shall be left alone if I do not make myself heard;" and as he rose to the summit of a sea, he shouted out with might and main, "*Lilly* ahoy!"

"Hold fast!" cried the captain. "Down with the helm again!" and then came a hearty cheer from the deck of the ship.

It convinced him that his voice had been heard, but now he had a long long time to wait. He was sure that a boat was being lowered, but sometimes he pictured her to himself swamped alongside, and perhaps all those coming to his rescue cast into the foaming sea. Anxiously he looked out for her. How long it had seemed since he had shouted, and yet no help had come to him. His confidence in his captain, however, was unabated. He was sure that help would come, sooner or later. All he had to do was to float till then. Fortunately, he did not think of sharks, but still more fortunately, the sharks did not think of him. At length he saw a dark object between him and the ship. Yes! Yes! It was a boat! Now it was hid from his sight. Now he saw it again.

"*Lilly* ahoy!" he shouted out again, but not so loud as before.

"Hurrah!" some voices cried in return;—"Cheer up, lad, cheer up; it's all right!"

And then he saw without doubt a boat approaching, now making her way on the summit of a foaming sea, now again sinking into the trough, and being hid from his view. Still on she came towards him.

"Cheer up, lad!" again shouted a voice. It was that of old Grim. He was sure he knew it.

At length there was the boat quite close to him. Eager hands were ready to grasp him, but there was the danger of being struck by the bows of the boat, or the oars.

He watched his opportunity, and singing out, "I'll make for the bow," he struck forward.

Grimshaw's arms were extended towards him, and in another instant he found himself grasped by those friendly hands, and hauled up into the boat.

"Why, the lad's as slippery as an eel!" cried old Grim. "Are you hurt, Bill?"

"No, thank you," answered Bill. "I'm hearty and strong, as if I had only been taking a swim for pleasure."

"We must put you aft, though, and a jacket over you," said old Grim.

Fortunately, one of the men had one on. It was off in a moment, and wrapped round Bill, who was passed aft into the stern-sheets.

"Thank Heaven you are saved, boy. The captain will be glad to hear it," said Mr Collinson, as he was putting the boat's head round.

And now once more she made for the ship. Bill was quickly hauled up the side.

"Gripe him hard!" sung out old Grim, "or he will slip through your fists, lads; he's got such a lot of seaweed round him."

"Why, how is this?" exclaimed the captain, as he saw Bill's condition.

Bill told him.

"You did wisely, lad," he observed; "and now go below and turn into your hammock, and I will send the doctor and a stiff glass of grog, if he will let you have it."

In another minute Bill was between the blankets; but the doctor, after feeling his pulse, pronounced him none the worse for his ducking. The grog came out hissing hot from the captain's cabin, but old Grim, who was standing by the boy's hammock, declared it was somewhat too stiff for a youngster, and helped him with half the contents; for which kindness Bill was none the worse.

When Bill came on deck, the sun was shining brightly, the sea was blue and smooth, and the ship was running to the west, with studding-sails below and aloft.

"I told you so," said Bill to a remark of old Grim's. "There's the sun shining out as bright as ever, and, through the mercy of Him who looks after us poor sailors, not one of us has lost the number of his mess."

Chapter Seven

A blue canopy, undimmed by a single cloud, was spread over the bright, sparkling ocean, in the midst of which the graceful corvette, her snow-white canvas tapering upwards, glided towards the coast of Jamaica. Ahead was seen, rising out of the green plain, range above range of lofty blue mountains, appearing above the stratum of clouds which rolled along their precipitous sides, their steep cliffs descending abruptly to the ocean, while thick forests covered the more gentle slopes of the hills. In a short time, the white buildings of Port Royal were distinguished at the end of a narrow sandy spit overgrown with mangroves, well known as the Palisades. At the farther end of the spit was seen the white walls of Fort Morant, with a steep hill rising above it. Passing between the formidable ramparts of Fort Charles on one side, thickly studded with heavy ordnance, and of Fort Augusta, with Rock Fort above it, capable of sinking any fleet which might have ventured to enter, the corvette ran on towards Kingston, where she brought up at some distance from the town.

"Well, this is a beautiful country!" exclaimed Bill, as he surveyed the scene in which he found himself. "It beats Portsmouth Harbour hollow—that it does, I'm sure."

"Just wait a bit till we have had yellow Jack aboard!" growled out old Grim. "Very fine to look at, maybe, but you will find it very different when you know it as well as I do. Once I belonged to a ship out in these parts, when we lost the better half of our ship's company before we got home again."

"I hope we shall be more fortunate," said Bill. "But what do you mean by yellow Jack?"

"The yellow fever, to be sure, boy. You will see a fellow one hour rolling along with a quid in his mouth, as happy as a prince, and the next down with the fever, and wriggling about with pain; and in the morning when you ask after him, if he's on shore, you will hear he is buried already; if he's at sea, the sailmaker will be busy sewing him up in his hammock."

When Bill went to the cabin to attend to his duties, the officers were all talking away of what they were going to do on shore. While dinner was going forward, Bill could not help hearing their conversation. Some of them were talking of friends they expected to find; others were proposing rides up the country to Rock Fort, and other places; some talked of going over to Spanish Town, the capital of the island.

"Well, Collinson, and do you expect to find your friends the Lydalls here?" asked Mr Barker.

"He wouldn't be looking so happy if he did not," said the master.

"I am not surprised at it," observed the surgeon. "I once saw Miss Ellen Lydall, and if I had not happened to have a wife and small family of my own, I should have been entering the lists with him myself."

"Colonel Lydall told me that he expected his regiment would be sent here. The colonel's family accompanied him out, and I hope to find that he is stationed either at Uphill Barracks or Rock Fort," answered Lieutenant Collinson.

"But I say, Collinson, do you think the young lady will have remained faithful all this time? Remember what numbers of soldier-officers and rich planters there are out here ready to supplant you. Ha! Ha! Ha!" and the purser laughed and rubbed his hands at his own joke.

Lieutenant Collinson took this bantering very coolly. "A man may take from messmates what he certainly would not from other persons," he answered.

Bill heard the remark, but very wisely never repeated out of the cabin what he heard in it. He did, however, think to himself, "Mr Collinson is a kind, good officer, and I only hope, if he likes this Miss Lydall, that he will fall in with her, and maybe marry her one of these days."

As the ship lay some way from the town, it was too late for any of the officers to go on shore that night. When dinner was over, and Bill had finished his duties in the gun-room, he went on deck, but found Tommy Rebow and some of the other lads skylarking about the fore-rigging. He soon joined them.

"Hillo, youngster!" cried Grimshaw, as he passed him. "Take care you don't fall overboard again. You will not come off as easily as you did before. Look out there! What do you say to that chap?" and old Grim pointed to a dark triangular object which was slowly gliding by the ship. "Do you know what that is?"

"No," said Bill, "I cannot make it out."

"Then I'll tell you," said old Grim. "That's Black Tom—the biggest shark in these seas. This harbour is his home; and he takes precious good care that no seaman shall swim ashore from his ship. He would be down upon him in a twinkling, if he caught him in the water. They say the Government keeps him in its pay to act watchman, and he goes up to the Dockyard to be fed every day."

Bill now distinguished a large black body beneath the fin, but it soon passed ahead of the ship and was lost to sight.

The next day Mr Collinson sent for Bill, and told him to clean himself and get ready to go with him on shore, to carry his carpet-bag. Bill was very quickly ready, and took charge of the bag, which the lieutenant's servant gave him. The purser, and master, and two or three midshipmen were going on shore at the same time. "Now," thought Bill, "I shall hear all about the young lady, for I dare say Mr Collinson is going up to look after her."

They passed several other ships of war, for it was a busy time then in the West Indies; for, though England had thrashed most of her enemies, there were still a number of privateers cruising about, and doing all the mischief they could. Captain Trevelyan expected to be employed in looking after them. He had already gone ashore in his gig to pay his respects to the admiral up at the Penn—as the residence of the commander-in-chief is called—situated on an elevation about two miles out of Kingston.

As soon as they landed, Mr Collinson, telling Bill to follow him, took leave of his companions, they casting knowing glances after him.

"Lucky fellow!" said one of the midshipmen. "Depend upon it he is all right, or he would not look so happy."

They soon learned that Colonel Lydall's regiment was stationed at Uphill Barracks. As it was too far to walk, he ordered a calêche, and directed Bill to put in his bag. Bill looked very much disappointed, thinking he should have to go back to the boat. Great was his pleasure, therefore, when the lieutenant said—

"Jump up behind, lad." And away they drove through the regular, broad streets of Kingston, and were soon ascending the hill towards the barracks.

It was a grand scene—the blue mountains rising up in a semicircle before them, with lofty groves of palmetto, the wild cotton-tree and fig-tree at their bases; behind them the clean-looking white town with the vast harbour beyond; the palisades stretching away on one side, with Port Royal at the end, separating it from the ocean; the merchant-vessels floating in the harbour of Kingston, while farther off were seen the lofty masts and spars of the men-of-war. It was very hot, but Bill did not mind the heat, and only wished the drive was to be longer. They were soon among the well-built airy barracks of Uphill Park camp, and Bill felt very grand as the carriage drove up to the officers' quarters.

"Now I hope I shall see this young lady Lieutenant Collinson thinks so much about," thought Bill to himself.

The lieutenant jumped from the carriage, and eagerly went to the hall-door. He came back, however, very soon, looking somewhat disappointed, and told the negro driver to go on farther up the country. Bill, however, was not sorry, as he thus had an opportunity of seeing more of the island.

"I hope the lady is there, however," he said to himself.

They drove on along the fine road, and among curious trees such as Bill had never seen in his life. There was the graceful bamboo, with its long leaves waving in the breeze; and the trumpet tree, from thirty to forty feet high, its trunk something like that of the bamboo, with a curious fruit growing on it not unlike the strawberry. Bill was quite delighted when he caught sight of a monkey leaping among the branches of a tree, wild and at liberty, like a squirrel in England. Away it went, however, as the carriage approached, stopping only now and then to have a look at the approaching vehicle, then hiding itself among the foliage.

At length, after driving some miles, ascending higher and higher, the carriage turned off towards a large cottage-looking building on the side of the hill. There was a broad verandah in front, looking out over the plain towards the sea beyond. Under the verandah, several ladies and gentlemen were collected.

Two or three blacks came out to meet the carriage, and the lieutenant, having exchanged a few words with them, proceeded across the garden to the verandah. Bill could just see a young lady, who had been seated with her back to the drive, start up as the lieutenant approached, and put out her hand to shake his, as he came up. A fine-looking gentleman, whom Bill took to be the colonel, advanced from the other end of the verandah, and seemed to welcome him warmly. He then saw him bow to the rest of the company, and finally shake hands with one or two whom he appeared to recognise.

"It's all right," said Bill.

Bill was soon at home among the negro servants. He did not turn up his nose at them because they were black, and was ready to laugh and joke with them, and help them in anything they were about. He was very glad when, after some time, the lieutenant told him to take the bag out of the carriage, for he was going to stop there that evening.

Old Sally, the black cook, especially took a great fancy to Bill, and he seldom had had so luxurious a dinner as she put before him.

"Dare, sailor-boy! Eat and grow fat. Dat better than salt junk dat dey give on board ship."

Bill, in return, danced a hornpipe for the amusement of his black friends, who stood round him grinning from ear to ear, and clapping their hands with delight, one or two of the negro boys trying to imitate him, though Sally and the rest declared that they could in no way come up to his performance.

When the colonel's party went to dinner, Bill was told to go in and help. This he was glad to do, as he thus had an opportunity of seeing the young lady he had heard spoken about.

Lieutenant Collinson was seated by her side. He was sure that must be she, from the way the lieutenant was speaking to her.

"Well," thought Bill, "no wonder Mr Collinson admires her. She is indeed a sweet young lady; so fair, and such blue eyes! And I think she seems pleased to have the lieutenant where he is."

Little, probably, did either the officer or the young lady dream of the thoughts which were entering Bill Sunnyside's head. There were a number of other guests present,—two or three officers of the regiment, a planter or two, as the West Indian proprietors are called, and several ladies. Bill, however, thought that the colonel's daughter surpassed them all. How very happy she looked, as the lieutenant spoke to her; her countenance varying according to the subject, often a rich glow overspreading her face, while her eyes flashed and sparkled. Certainly, if the lieutenant had cared for her before, he must have admired her now more than ever. And so he did,— of that there could be little doubt; and he would have been ready at any moment to give his life for hers, and to fight to the last gasp to defend her from danger.

Chapter Eight

After spending a couple of days at Rockhill Cottage (for that was the name of the colonel's residence), Lieutenant Collinson, accompanied by Bill, returned on board. Each time, however, that the lieutenant went to the colonel's house he took Bill with him, who, accordingly, found himself thoroughly at home there. Sally especially won his affections. She sometimes in her kindness reminded him of his mother, only she was a great deal larger and fatter, and her skin was very black. "But, after all," as Bill observed, "what has that to do with it? It's the heart that I am talking about, the nature of which just comes out through the eyes and acts; and even mother could not be much kinder than Sally sometimes is, though, to be sure, she can knock the black boys about pretty smartly; but then maybe they deserve it, and their heads are somewhat thick, so that they don't feel when she comes down with a frying-pan on the top of them."

At length the corvette got put to rights; and stores and provisions having been taken on board, the admiral ordered her away on a cruise.

Mr Collinson looked somewhat sad when he bade Miss Ellen Lydall farewell.

"We shall be back soon, however," he said.

He did his best to keep up his spirits; and he told the young lady to do the same. As the carriage drove off, Bill saw her watching it, and she did not move from the point of the garden which commanded the road as long as it was in sight.

The *Lilly* was to be some time absent:—to proceed to the westward, and then to come round the northern coast of Cuba, in search of the privateers, which were an excessive annoyance to the English merchantmen passing through those seas. They had been at sea some days, and had seen no vessels.

"Well, Grimshaw," said Bill, "you see we have not had yellow Jack aboard yet, and I hope, in spite of what you have said, he will not pay us a visit."

"Don't sing out yet, Master Bill," answered old Grim. "Just stay till we have been into some of the harbours we shall have to visit, or been becalmed for a week together, with the water in the tank so hot that it pretty well scalds your mouth to drink it, and no need of a fire in the galley, because as how we can cook the meat by just hanging it up in the sun."

Bill laughed. "It must be pretty hot for that," he observed; "and I didn't expect we should have it much hotter than we have had it already."

"Wait a bit, boy, wait a bit," answered Grimshaw. "Now, you youngsters, what are you skylarking away there for?" he shouted out to several of the lads, who were, as usual, in spite of the hot sun, frolicking about in the rigging, accompanied by Queerface, the monkey.

Just as he spoke, Tommy Rebow was hunting the animal from shroud to backstay, up over the mast-head and down again. At last, Master Queerface made a spring out on the fore-yard. Tommy pursued him with thoughtless eagerness, and, in his attempt to get hold of him, lost his grasp. Over he went. In vain he caught at the foot-rope; and giving a turn, struck the water with his head. Down beneath the surface he went. Bill saw him falling, and knew well he could not swim. In spite of old Grim's caution about the sharks, without a moment's hesitation in he plunged, and swam towards the spot where Tommy had gone down.

"A man overboard! A man overboard!" was shouted by numbers who saw the accident.

The corvette was going at the rate of only three or four knots through the water. Bill swam rapidly on, his eye fixed on the centre of the circle made by Tommy as he fell.

"He's gone! He's gone!" shouted out several voices from the ship. Tommy, however, quickly again came to the surface, and Bill caught him as he appeared.

"A shark! A shark!" cried several voices.

Among the first who saw the shark was Jack Windy. He had a large knife in his hand, employed in some work, and, without waiting to cry out, overboard he went, and swam up to where the boys were struggling in the water. Old Grimshaw at the moment saw the danger of his young friend, and not knowing what Jack was about, overboard he went, with a boat's stretcher in his hand, purporting to do battle with the monster. At that instant the captain came on deck.

"Who's overboard?" he asked.

"Bill Sunnyside—Sunshine Bill, sir," cried out several voices.

"The lad whom I promised his widowed mother to protect," thought the captain, for he scarcely uttered the words aloud.

He had on a light silk jacket. There was no necessity to throw that off, but taking his watch out of his pocket, he handed it to one of the midshipmen, and, in another instant, he also was overboard, and swimming away towards Bill and Tommy.

"Turn on your back, Tommy!" cried Bill. "If you catch me round the neck, we shall both be drowned."

Tommy was too much frightened to understand what Bill said. The latter had, therefore, to tear himself from his grasp, and to swim away a little distance, only to return, however, to seize him by the collar.

The monster of the deep during this time had been eyeing the human beings in the water. Had there been only one, he would have attacked him immediately; but the number of persons swimming about made him somewhat timid. Jack, seeing that Bill was handling Tommy scientifically, kept his eye on the spot where he had seen the shark.

"Come on," he shouted, when he saw Grimshaw in the water; "we two will tackle the brute. And here comes our skipper, God bless him! He will look after the boys."

Mr Barker meantime had hove the ship to, and a boat was lowered, into which Mr Collinson had leaped with four hands, who were pulling with all their might towards the spot, though of course they had by this time some distance to go.

The captain swam on towards Bill and Tommy, and came up just as the latter had got Bill a second time round the throat.

Those on board had been watching Jack with intense anxiety. Once the monster was seen to be darting towards the captain, but, as he approached, Jack struck out towards him with his knife in his hand, while Grimshaw beat the water with his stick. The effect was to startle the shark. Jack dived; but, to the horror of all, a patch of blood appeared on the surface directly afterwards. None expected to see Jack Windy again. The next instant, however, up he came, shouting out—

"I've done for him! I've done for him!"

Meantime, Grimshaw was swimming round and round where the boys and the captain were, shouting, and kicking, and beating the water, which he continued to do till the boat came up to the spot.

"Take in the boys and the captain," he shouted out; "we will hold our own against the sharks."

There was little time to be lost, however, for the monster defeated by Jack was not the only one. Several others, attracted by the blood of their companion, came swimming swiftly towards the spot. The captain and the two boys were quickly hauled on board. Grimshaw was taken in next, and Jack had only just time to draw in his legs, before a huge shark, turning up the white of its belly, appeared close to the side of the boat.

"If I had been ready for you, you would have repented your boldness, Master Shark," cried Jack, as he saw the monster retreat, disappointed of its prey.

At first the captain thought that it was Bill who had first tumbled overboard; but when he found that he had leaped in to save Tommy Rebow, he praised him greatly; and from that day Bill became even a greater favourite than before with all on board. Sometimes prosperity spoils people. It was not the case with Sunshine Bill.

The ship had been at sea for some weeks, beating to the westward, when she rounded Cape Saint Antonio, the western coast of Cuba, and stood towards the coast of Florida. At length, one morning at daybreak, two vessels were seen about four miles away to the southward. One was a brig, the other a schooner.

The *Lilly* instantly made sail towards them, setting all the canvas she could spread. As soon as she was seen, the schooner made sail, evidently to escape her. The breeze freshened, and she was soon up with the brig, which was seen to be an English merchant-vessel. As they passed her a voice hailed—

"We have been plundered by a privateer or pirate, and should have had our throats cut, had not you come up."

"We will return to you as soon as we can catch her," answered Captain Trevelyan, not wishing to run the risk of losing the privateer by heaving-to at that time.

Accordingly, the *Lilly* stood on. Though the schooner was a fast vessel, the *Lilly*, bringing up the breeze, was quickly overhauling her. As the corvette drew near, the schooner was seen to have her decks crowded with men; and presently, to show that she was not about to yield without a struggle, a couple of shot were fired from her after-guns. They were evidently aimed with the hopes of cutting away some of the *Lilly's* rigging. The corvette replied with her bowchasers, the schooner firing again and again in return.

Several of the best marksmen on board tried their hands, in the hopes of knocking away some of the schooner's rigging instead. At length Mr Collinson stepped up to the gun. He fired, and down came the schooner's mainsail. He had shot away the jaws of the maingaff.

A shout rose from the deck of the English ship. On she stood, with her broadside ready to rake her antagonist, who had fallen off before the wind. Just as she was about to deliver her fire, a man jumped into the main rigging and shouted out—

"We surrender!" the French flag having already come down with the peak.

"Lower your sails, then, and we will send a boat on board," cried Captain Trevelyan.

Mr Collinson instantly jumped into the boat which was lowered, and boarded the schooner. Her crew were a motley set of Frenchmen, Spaniards, mulattoes, and blacks. They cast anything but pleasant looks at their captors, and it was very evident that if they had dared they would have hove them quickly overboard again.

Mr Collinson having received the sword of their commander, ordered them to prepare to quit the vessel. The other boats of the corvette were very quickly alongside with armed crews, who began at once to remove the people from the prize. When the greater number were conveyed on board the corvette, the captain told Mr Collinson to take charge of the schooner with a prize crew, and to carry her round to Jamaica. The lieutenant received the order with no little satisfaction, hoping that he should thus again have an opportunity of renewing his visits at Rock Hill Cottage.

Chapter Nine

The prize was called the *Flèche*, belonging to Dominique. Mr Collinson having to select a crew, among others took Jack Windy, Grimshaw, and Bill, and Tommy Rebow to attend in the cabin; having, besides, a mate and a midshipman to act as his officers. The corvette could ill spare so many men, but the prize was a valuable one, and it was important to take her into Port Royal in safety.

On reaching the brig, it was found that the schooner had taken a considerable amount of property from her, though prevented by the appearance of the corvette from removing much of her cargo. The captain of the brig was very grateful for his release, and went rejoicing on his voyage, hoping not to fall in with a similar customer. The *Flèche*, under her new officers and crew, stood away to the westward, hoping, after rounding Cape Saint Antonio, to have a quick run to Jamaica, while the corvette continued her voyage through the Bahama sea, towards Saint Domingo.

For some time the schooner enjoyed fine weather, and everybody on board was happy and contented, imitating the temper of the lieutenant, who was especially so.

Bill, under Jack Windy's instruction, perfected himself in his hornpipe, and Jack declared, and even old Grim growled out an assent, that there were not many lads of his age who could beat him. The wind was very light, so that, after having parted from the corvette some four or five days, they had made but little way. Bill, of course, had a very slight idea all the time where they were, for charts and maps were not common between-decks. They had been on board the schooner some ten days or more, when the weather began to cloud over, and just the same appearance came on which Bill remembered before the hurricane they had met with on their passage from England.

"What do you think of it?" he asked of old Grim.

"Why, if Mr Collinson don't look out bright, we shall have the masts out of the ship, that's all," answered Grim.

Mr Collinson was, however, looking out bright, and soon summoned on deck by the mate who had charge, he gave orders to furl all sail, except a close-reefed fore-topsail. There was not a breath of wind. The sea was like a looking-glass, the heat was intense.

"No doubt it's old 'Harry Cane,' come to pay us a visit, as he's not got the change out of us yet," growled old Grim.

The lieutenant and his two young officers walked the deck, looking somewhat anxiously.

"There are some ugly rocks and banks clustering pretty thickly about here," he observed to one of them, "and if we have to run on in the dark, Providence alone can take us clear of them."

"I would rather trust to Providence than to our own wisdom or skill," thought Bill. "He who took care of us before will take care of us now."

Some time passed, and still the calm continued. Even Mr Collinson began to think that, after all, the hurricane was not coming.

"Don't let him fancy any such thing," observed old Grim. "Depend upon it, if 'Harry Cane' has made up his mind to come aboard us, come he will; but whether or no he will take the masts out of us, or send us to the bottom, is another thing."

The sky still remained overcast, and the heat increased. The men were piped to dinner, and many a joke was cut at the mess-tables about the expected hurricane.

"Oh! It's only a make-believe, after all," observed Jack Windy, as he tossed off his grog, dinner being over.

The men had not left their seats, when, on a sudden, a loud low roar was heard.

"All hands on deck!" shouted Mr Collinson.

"All hands on deck!" echoed the voice of the acting boatswain, piping shrilly as he spoke.

The men rushed from below. They had scarcely gained the deck, when that same frothy, hissing line of foam was seen advancing which had before been seen. Like a blow from a mallet, the gale struck the vessel. At first, she seemed to hesitate to move forward. Then she sprang on, and away she flew dead before it. On she went, the seas increasing rapidly as she advanced. In a short time, however, the wind shifted and caught the sail aback. The schooner seemed about to make a stern-board. Before the order could be given to let go the sheets, a loud thundering noise was heard like the report of a piece of ordnance, and the sail, blown from the bolt-ropes, flew away before the blast. The fore-staysail was run up, and once more the schooner's head was turned away before the wind. On again she flew in a different direction.

"It is as I feared," said Mr Collinson to the mate, Mr Tatham. "She is going right in among the rocks and shoals in the direction of the Tortugas."

There were no signs of the hurricane abating; indeed, it seemed wonderful that with the cross-breaking seas which raged round the vessel, she should not have been sent instantly to the bottom. Mr Collinson and the mate were at the helm. Jack Windy was stationed to look out ahead — not that looking out would do any good. The schooner flew on. Night was approaching. Darkness added horror to the scene. Even the oldest seaman felt his heart sinking, and his cheek paler than usual.

Sunshine Bill knew as well as any one the danger the schooner was in, but he said to himself, "This is what seamen have to go through, and He who saved us before can find a way now for us to escape, even though coral reefs or rocky islands are ahead."

The crew kept at their stations. No one felt inclined to go below. Like true British seamen, they determined boldly to face the danger. Now and then there was a lull and hopes were entertained that the hurricane was breaking. It only seemed to be taking a rest to obtain fresh strength. Hour after hour the schooner flew on. Once or twice Mr Collinson went below to look at the chart, but he was quickly on deck again to resume his post.

"We must be in the midst of reefs and banks, Tatham," he observed. "Look out on the starboard bow there. See that wall of white? The sea is meeting with resistance there, depend on it."

Presently there was a cry forward —

"Breakers! Breakers on the starboard bow." The helm was put a-starboard, in the hopes of avoiding the reef.

"Breakers! Breakers ahead!" again shouted Jack Windy. "Breakers on the larboard bow!"

"Grimshaw, come and help Mr Tatham at the helm," shouted Mr Collinson; and he went forward, scanning the raging, breaking sea ahead.

Soon it seemed as if all around there was a semicircle of white foam, rising like a lofty wall to impede their progress. Just in one spot there appeared to be a break. He hurried aft and put the helm to port, boldly steering the schooner towards it.

Still there was but little hope. Destruction seemed to await the vessel and all on board. On, on she flew. In another instant there was a fearful crash, and the masts bent like willow wands. Over they went, carrying two poor fellows with them, whose death-shriek was heard above the roar of the breakers. Again the schooner struck. Another sea came roaring up astern, as if it would wash all from her decks and hurl them to destruction. The remainder of the crew clung to ring-bolts or stanchions, or whatever they could grasp. The sea lifted the schooner and sent her farther on the reef. Again and again she struck, as if every timber was about to separate. Another sea roared up, and striking her like a huge hammer, broke her into a thousand fragments, sending those on board far into the water, clinging to the fragments. Happily she had been driven almost over the reef, on the inner side of which the sea was comparatively smooth. Thus those who had been clinging to portions of the wreck were able to support themselves.

Sunshine Bill had been holding on to a ring-bolt in the deck, and when the ship broke up, he found himself still doing so, and floating on a portion of it which had been sent a considerable distance from the reef. He looked around him to see if any of his shipmates had also escaped immediate destruction. As far as he could see, the water seemed covered with pieces of timber, which were torn off from the wreck. Among them he thought he could distinguish some human forms. He shouted. A voice answered him: it was that of Tommy Rebow, close to him, floating on a fragment of the bulwarks.

"Oh! Help me, Bill! Help me! I cannot hold on much longer, and the piece of wood I have hold of is scarcely enough to keep me afloat."

Bill felt tolerably secure where he was, yet he could not bear the thoughts of letting Tommy perish if he could help him; so, leaving his own piece of the wreck, he struck out towards his messmate. He fortunately had not many yards to go before he got up with Tommy.

"Hold on," he said, "and I'll tow your raft up to mine. I don't want to run the risk of letting you catch me round the neck as you did the other day. But cheer up; I don't think we're going to die this time."

With these encouraging words, Bill towed Tommy up to the piece of deck, which was amply large enough to support them both. Having got on it himself, he managed, though not without difficulty, to hand Tommy up also, and there together they clung to the ring-bolt.

"I wonder who else has escaped?" said Bill. "I'll shout out. Listen if anybody answers."

Even to Tommy, Bill found it necessary to speak very loud, on account of the roar of the breakers, which seemed even louder on that side of the reef than on the other.

"Anybody floating away there?" shouted Bill, his shrill voice being heard above the dull roar of the ocean. "Hark! I hear two or three voices replying," said Bill. "Let's give them a cheer, to keep up their spirits; perhaps they will come and join us here. I do hope Mr Collinson has escaped, and Jack Windy, and poor old Grim, and the other fellows too. Yes, I am nearly certain that is Jack's voice."

"Is there room for anybody else where you are?"

"Yes!" shouted Bill and Tommy. "Plenty for you, if you will come to us."

In a short time Jack managed to swim up to the raft. It was very evident that it had been drifting still farther away from the reef. They helped Jack up as he reached the raft, considerably exhausted by his swim.

"We have got inside a lagoon," he observed when he was seated on deck. "If it had not been for that, we should all have been dead by this time. But I have some hopes that others may have escaped. Look away down there to leeward. Can't you see something rising up against the sky? They look to me like cocoa-nut trees, and I should not be surprised if there's an island down there, and that, if we are in luck, we shall be landed on it before the night is over."

Bill thought with Jack that he could see trees.

"Well," he said, "we at all events have to be thankful; but I do hope Mr Collinson has escaped. What would that poor young lady do if he was drowned? I should not like to go back to Jamaica to have to tell her. Dear me! It makes my heart bleed to think of it."

"I can't help thinking that there are some other people down away there, holding on to other pieces of the wreck," said Jack; "but, you see, the breakers make such a roar that 'tis hard to hear a hail at any distance. I only just heard your's and Tommy's squeaking voices, and I was not half as far off as those pieces of the wreck are. Well, it's an awful scene. I never saw a vessel go to pieces so quickly before; but then, to be sure, it's not often a craft gets such tremendous blows as she did. Nothing made of wood and iron could have held together, I am sure, on that reef."

While Jack was making these remarks, he was looking out to try and get some smaller pieces of timber to serve, he said, as paddles. At length they came up with a floating spar—for it must be understood that they were moving faster through the water than the other pieces of wreck, owing to their bodies holding the wind and serving as sails. Jack managed to secure this prize, and Bill directly afterwards got hold of a piece of board. As the water was smoother the farther they got away from the reef, they were the better able to use these paddles, not being obliged to cling any longer to the ring-bolt. As they advanced, the shadowy forms of the trees appeared before them, becoming at length sufficiently distinct to assure them that an island was at no great distance. A surf, however, broke on the shore, though it did not appear to be very dangerous. They could just see a sandy beach, a few feet high only, with a grove of tall trees. At length, hurried on by the gale, and by their own exertions, the raft reached the beach, when a sea striking it washed them off, though happily they were thrown sufficiently high up the sand to enable them to gain their feet and scramble up out of the way of the succeeding sea.

Sunshine Bill did not forget to whom he was indebted for his preservation, and falling on his knees, to the surprise of his companions, he offered up a short thanksgiving for his safety.

"And I am sure we ought to be thankful too," said Jack, imitating his example.

"And I wish you would just say a word for me," said Tommy. "I am not much accustomed to pray—I never learnt."

"Oh! Tommy," said Bill, "it doesn't require practice. God doesn't care about the words. Just thank Him from your heart, and never mind how you speak your thanks."

"I say, Jack, let us look out and see if we cannot help some of the other fellows," said Bill, as he rose from his knees. "Maybe they will come ashore more exhausted than we are, and perhaps not be able to help themselves out of the water."

Jack and the two boys stood looking out over the lagoon. They could see the white wall of foam as it rose over the reef, and between it and them could distinguish several floating objects, but whether human beings or pieces of the wreck, it was hard to tell.

Chapter Ten

Sunshine Bill and his two companions stood for some time watching the objects they had seen floating in the lagoon.

"Yes, I'm sure there's a man there!" exclaimed Bill. "Let us shout to him: he will hear us, maybe, and it will keep up his spirits."

They raised their voices in a hearty cheer. A faint answer came back.

"I thought so," cried Bill; "but the man, whoever he is, must be tired, and the cheer did him good. I have a great mind to go off and help him on shore."

"No, no, Bill," said Jack, "I'll do that. I am stronger than you are, and we cannot afford to risk losing you."

Saying this, Jack, rushing into the water, boldly swam off through the surf towards the man they had seen. He soon got up to him, but only just in time to find him relaxing his hold of the timber he had been clinging to.

"Come, mate, whoever you are," said Jack, as he saw him; "hold on, and I'll help tow you ashore."

Bill and Tommy ran into the surf to help them as they landed. The other man was so exhausted that he could scarcely lift himself on his feet.

"It's old Grim!" cried Bill, as he saw him. "Well, I am glad he has escaped."

Tommy made them no answer, as he had not forgotten the many rope's-endings old Grim had from time to time given him. They got him up and seated him on the beach. He soon recovered his strength sufficiently to speak.

"Thank you, mates, thank you," he growled out. "And I say, Bill, I told you ill-luck was coming. What have you got to say to it?"

"That I am very thankful we have escaped with our lives," answered Bill. "And so we ought to be; and I have no doubt that He who has helped us thus far will help us still farther. That is all I have got to say now. But hurrah! Surely there's somebody else floating out there on a bit of timber. Jack, look! I am right, am I not?"

"Yes, Bill, and I wish I was a better swimmer than I am; I would go off and help him. But old Grim cost me a good tussle, and I don't feel quite as if I could manage it again just now."

Jack, in truth, had been considerably exhausted in coming through the surf, and had now to sit down and rest himself. Meantime they kept watching the surface of the lagoon, in the hopes that more of their shipmates might have escaped. Bill was most concerned about Mr Collinson.

"Oh dear! Oh dear! If he should be drowned," he said to himself over and over again. "That poor young lady! It will break her heart—I know it will, for all that she looked so bright and spirited." Suddenly Bill started up. "Come along, Tommy; come along, Jack. I am sure I heard a shout a little way along the shore. It is there where the pieces of wreck are now drifting."

Grimshaw was too tired to move, but Jack and Tommy followed Bill, who ran along the beach to a point towards which a large bit of timber was drifting. There was a man on it. He again shouted as they approached.

"Ay, ay! We'll help you!" cried Bill.

Probably the man dreaded, should he continue to cling to the pieces of wreck, that when he touched the beach it might roll over him.

"Leave it and swim!" cried Jack.

The man did so, and he and Bill rushed into the water, and just as the sea was carrying him off again, caught hold of his hands and dragged him up in time to escape the timber, which was cast with violence directly afterwards on to the beach.

"Hurrah! I am so glad!" cried Bill, for he recognised in the rescued man his kind friend—Lieutenant Collinson.

Mr Collinson was very much exhausted, and for some time after he had been assisted up to a dry place on the shore, was unable to speak. At length he told them that he had been endeavouring to help some of his companions, but in vain, and that he feared greatly all the rest were lost. He seemed much out of spirits.

"We did all we could," he said, "and may be thankful that our lives are so far spared. When daylight returns, we may ascertain where we are; but

I am afraid we are on one of the small islets of these seas, which afford no water, nor means of supporting life."

"We will hope for the best, sir," said Bill. "And perhaps we may catch some fish, or some provisions may be washed on shore; and as for water, if we cannot find a spring, maybe the clouds will send it to us."

"You set a good example of confidence in God's mercy," observed the lieutenant.

"Yes, sir, I am sure He never forgets us; and so while there's life there's hope, for even at the last He may send us help."

In vain the party looked out in the hopes of more of their shipmates being driven on shore. Once they thought they heard a cry as if some poor fellow had let go his hold of the plank to which he was clinging, but though almost wearied to death, they would not lie down, lest by so doing they might fail to rescue any who might still be alive. At length they had to give up all hopes of saving more lives, and went and laid themselves down under a clump of trees near the beach. All the party, with the exception of the lieutenant, were soon asleep. He sat up, thinking probably of those far away, and wishing that he could give notice to his friends at Jamaica of his safety.

"When the corvette gets back, and it is found that the schooner has not arrived, it will be supposed that we are all lost. Ellen will be grieving for me, poor girl, and what would I not do to shield her from a minute's pain or suffering?" he thought.

At length, however, he followed the example of his companions, and also, in spite of his anxiety, fell fast asleep. When morning dawned, the gale had altogether ceased. The sea was blue and shining, the lagoon calm almost as a mirror. The whole shore was strewn with pieces of the wreck and portions of the cargo. The party were soon on their feet. The place on which they had been thrown was a small islet, scarcely more than fifty yards wide, and five or six hundred long; a group of trees, a few bushes, and a sprinkling of coarse grass being the only vegetation upon it. The whole sea, as far as the eye could reach, was covered with similar islets, few of them of larger dimensions, while some were smaller, mere rocks rising out of the ocean. The difficulty of escaping from such a place was very great, as no vessels were likely to pass near so dangerous a portion of the sea, while the island afforded no means of building a boat, nor of supporting existence. As soon as the lieutenant had aroused himself, however, he directed his four companions to accompany him to the beach, that they might look for whatever had been thrown on shore. Eagerly they searched on either side. At length Bill espied a cask. They hurried towards it, and dragged it up out of the reach of the water.

"It looks as if it had beef or pork in it," observed old Grim; "but unless we can get some biscuit and some water, it won't do us much good, as I can tell you from experience."

"But what do you think of this cask?" cried Bill, running on a little farther. "This is bread—I am sure of it by its looks. Maybe we shall get some water too. We have no cause to complain. See! Here's a chest, too. It's the carpenter's; and if we put our hands to the work, perhaps we shall be able to build a boat, or raft of some sort, and get to the mainland."

Numerous other articles were found and hauled up. Still no casks of water—the great want of all—had been discovered. They had been labouring for some time, having already collected a number of articles, when Tommy caught sight of several objects floating round the farther end of the island at no great distance from the shore. He shouted out to his companions, and they all ran in that direction. They were soon seen to be casks, mixed up with pieces of the wreck. The difficulty, however, was to get hold of them before they were swept away.

"If we could but make a bit of a raft, now," said Jack, "I would not mind going out with a paddle and bringing them in."

No sooner was the proposal made, than all hands set to work to build a light raft, for which there were ample materials. Bill volunteered to help Jack, and with the aid of a couple of roughly constructed paddles, they went off towards the casks.

"They are water-casks! No doubt about that," cried Jack, as he got near to them; "but whether they have fresh or salt water in them remains to be proved."

"Fresh water!" cried Bill; "let us hope so, at all events."

Having brought some rope on their raft, they made the casks fast and towed them towards the beach. There were three. They considerably impeded the return of the raft to the shore. Still Jack and Bill persevered. It was very hard work, as there was a current against them. However, they determined to persevere as long as they should make way. The casks were too precious to be abandoned, so they kept on paddling and paddling.

Sometimes Jack thought they were going farther off from the shore. "Keep on!" cried Bill. "We have gained an inch, and in another minute we shall have gained two inches. Hurrah!"

Jack was inspirited by Bill's courage, and after a great deal of exertion they managed to get the raft to the shore, their friends hurrying down to meet them. The casks were dragged up. As they turned them round, they saw that the bungs were fastened down tightly. Before they could get them open they had recourse to the carpenter's chest. The difficulty, however, was to open that. They searched about in vain for any implement to force it open. They were, however, so thirsty that they could wait no longer, and at length, by means of a stick and a piece of timber to serve as a mallet, they drove in the bung. How eagerly they drew forth the water from the cask! Jack put down his mouth and tasted it.

"Sweet as honey!" he exclaimed. "No fear now; if all the casks are like that, we shall do."

"But it's not likely they will be all like that," said old Grim. "How that one has escaped is more than I can tell."

The water greatly revived them. In the same way they knocked in the head of one of the casks which contained biscuit. It was found to have escaped the wet. All hands eagerly ate some, for they had tasted no food for many hours. Here was an ample supply to last them for some time. Greatly refreshed, with their spirits somewhat raised, they again went along the shore to try and pick up any further article that might be of use. Among others, Tommy found a saucepan with the lid firmly on. It had floated unharmed towards the island. This was eagerly secured. They had now the means of cooking their meat and boiling water.

"Oh! Bill, what is that?" exclaimed Tommy, pointing to a distance along the beach. "There's a poor fellow, but he must be dead, I'm afraid."

The boys hurried towards the man. He was perfectly dead; of that there was no doubt. They drew the body, however, out of the water, and in doing so recognised him as one of the carpenter's crew.

"If he was alive, now, he would have assisted us," said Tommy, "in opening the chest and in building a boat. We will tell Mr Collinson, and he will have the poor fellow buried," observed Bill. "It may be difficult, though, to dig a grave in this thin coating of sand, with a hard rock below it. But hillo! What is here? See, Tommy; I have found this key fastened with a rope-yarn round his neck. I should not be surprised but what it's the key of the chest."

Saying this, and covering up the face of the dead man with his jacket, which they took off for the purpose, they hurried back to their companions. Sure enough, the key opened the carpenter's chest, and they had now the means of tapping the other casks, and of building themselves huts, if necessary. Still, though there was an abundance of timber from the wreck of the schooner, no one had sufficient skill to build a boat.

Chapter Eleven

Main was the search for water; though every inch of ground throughout the island was carefully surveyed, not a sign of a spring could be discovered.

Having examined all the provisions which had been collected, Mr Collinson found they had sufficient for two months or so, on short allowance. It might be managed so as to last rather longer; but could they hope to get away even in that time? Not only months, but years might go by, before any vessel might pass sufficiently near to distinguish them. They had no means of making a signal, for all the masts and spars had been carried away when the schooner first struck; and, being dashed about on the reef, had been broken to fragments. The group of trees were all close together, so that no signal could be seen flying from them.

Mr Collinson evidently had great difficulty in keeping up his own spirits; he did his best, however, for some time. Employment, he knew, was a great thing both for himself and the rest. He therefore advised that they should build a hut, which would shelter them from the heat in the day, and, should the rainy season come on, protect them from the rain. For this purpose there was an ample supply of timber. Having built the hut, they next began to furnish it. First, they made a table and stools. Jack Windy proposed, when the lieutenant was out of hearing, that they should make a chair for him. On this they all four set to work, and, whenever he was away, got on with it, putting it aside when he returned. In a couple of days, they had the satisfaction of presenting him with a comfortable armchair. It was evident, indeed, that he needed it, for, in spite of his courage, anxiety was preying upon him, and his health and strength were failing. Bill watched him anxiously.

"It will never do if he gives in," he said to himself, and he thought how he could best arouse him.

Whenever Mr Collinson was within hearing, Bill talked more cheerfully than ever.

"You said, sir, the other day, that we should have the rainy season down upon us before long; if so, we need not be afraid of want of water. I was looking at a place at the other end of the island, where there's a large piece of flat ground, and I thought to myself, if we could dig a hole in the middle, and just make some small trenches leading into it, when the rain comes down we might chance to get some water. Maybe it won't be very clean, but we could pass it through some sail-cloth, or some of the linen we found in the carpenter's chest, and so we shall be able to fill up our casks again."

"A very good idea," said Mr Collinson; "we will try it, at all events."

"And I was thinking, sir, that we might get some fish. I found a paper of fish-hooks in the chest, among other things; and there's no doubt we should find plenty of fish out in the lagoon."

"We will make a raft and try," said Mr Collinson. "I have been thinking of it, though, but I did not know any fish-hooks had been found."

"I used to be a capital hand at fishing, sir, in Portsmouth Harbour," said Bill, "and always had more luck than anybody else; so I hope I shall have here."

While the rest of the party were building a raft, Bill hunted along the shore, where he found several varieties of shell-fish.

"Some of these will help to keep us alive, if we cannot get fish," he observed, as he returned with them; "but I have no doubt that some of them will serve as bait; we will try, at all events."

Next morning, at daybreak, all hands were engaged in constructing a small raft capable of carrying two or three people. Some paddles were formed, and a mast and sail rigged, so that they might even go out as far as the reef. Some small line was found that served pretty well for fishing-lines, when Bill and Jack Windy, getting on the raft, paddled out to a little distance from the shore. Bill's line had not been in the water two minutes before he got a bite, and directly afterwards he hauled up a fine, big fish. In two or three minutes more he caught another; and, curiously enough, he had caught five, while Jack, who was on the other side of the raft, only caught one.

"Why, you are in luck, Bill," said Jack.

"I don't know how it is," said Bill, "but it's always the case with me. Whenever I used to go out fishing with anybody else, I always caught three times as many fish as they did. At all events, I am thankful that we have been so fortunate."

In an hour, the raft returned with fish enough to serve the party for a couple of days. Their success put them in good spirits, and even Mr Collinson revived greatly. A tinder-box having been found in the chest, they were able to light a fire to cook their fish. Some they boiled, and some they roasted on spits. Mr Collinson, however, who had been as a midshipman in the South Seas, recollected the way the natives of several islands cooked their fish. Having collected a number of leaves, the fish were wrapped up in them. A hole was then dug, and a number of stones, heated in the fire, were thrown into it. On the top of these the fish were placed. More leaves were then thrown in, and the whole covered in with earth.

Old Grim looked on with a considerable amount of doubt as to the success of the experiment exhibited in his countenance. Mr Collinson, however, told them that he would let them know when it was time to remove the earth. In about half an hour he came back, and the earth being cleared away and the leaves removed, steam arose from the hole, and the fish were found perfectly cooked and hot. The whole party agreed that they had never before tasted more delicious fish.

They had now no longer any fear of starving. Still, as Mr Collinson gazed over the ocean, he could not help feeling that they were thus only prolonging their lives to meet, ultimately, with the same termination.

"We shall soon be getting the scurvy among us," he thought to himself, "as no man can live on this diet, without vegetables, and escape that horrible complaint; and even if we do not get the scurvy, we must sink at last from want of water."

He also felt the life he was compelled to lead far more than did the others. They were companions to each, while he was, as it were, alone. Often and often he went away by himself to the other end of the island to consider by what means they could escape from their imprisonment. He did not forget also to lift up his heart in prayer for guidance and protection.

"God may find a way for us to escape, though I know not how it is to be," he said often to himself.

Thus day after day, and week after week, passed away. Although they had most carefully husbanded their water, it was now growing very scarce. Not a drop of rain had fallen by which it could be replenished.

They had wisely covered up the casks with planks and boughs, so as to keep them from the heat, and to diminish the evaporation as much as possible. Still, in that climate, a good deal of water, they knew, must thus be lost. From sunrise to sunset, their eyes were consequently cast over the ocean, in the hopes of discovering a sail; but none appeared, proving that Mr Collinson was right when he told them that few vessels were likely to pass that way. Still hope was kept alive in their bosoms.

As they saw the water decreasing, they now also began to look out eagerly for signs of rain; but the sky remained blue as ever, undimmed by a single cloud. Day after day the sun rose, and came burning down on their heads, to sink again into the same unclouded horizon. Their tank had long been formed. Bill especially made frequent visits to it, to keep it clean. He was more sanguine than the rest as to the advantage of the tank.

"I doubt, boy, in spite of all you say, if it will ever hold water, even if the rain does come down," said old Grim, in his usual tone. "We are all doomed men—that's my opinion. I may be wrong, of course; and I hope so for your sake, Bill. It's hard for a young chap like you to die; but for an old fellow like me, it's no odds to no one."

At length Mr Collinson, in spite of all his efforts to keep up, again overcome by weakness, was unable to leave the hut. Bill sat by his side, doing his utmost to cheer him. His favourite topic was the drive from Kingston to Rock Hill Cottage, and the pleasant days he had spent there.

"And, sir, I am very sure we shall be back there one of these days. I don't think, after we have been preserved so long, we shall be left to perish; though how we are to get away is more than I can say."

On examining the cask, Jack Windy discovered, however, on that very day, that scarcely two quarts of water remained.

"Sam Grimshaw," he said, addressing old Grim, as he pointed to the cask, "this is a bad job, but we must not let the lieutenant know of it. It will not do to give him less than his usual quantity; and you and I and the others must manage to go on still shorter commons."

Old Grim readily agreed to this, as did Bill and Tommy—the latter, perhaps, somewhat unwillingly. For several days, whenever the lieutenant, who was suffering from fever, asked for water, it was brought to him, though the brave fellows felt their own throats parched and dry, and would only allow themselves just enough to wet their lips whenever they could no longer bear the thirst.

At length but a pint remained; and with heavier hearts than usual they went to bed, feeling almost as if they could not hold out more than another day. Several times during the night, Bill got up to give Mr Collinson the water he asked for. It was a sore trial to him, yet he would not put the cup to his own lips, though, if his pocket had been full of gold, he would have given the whole of it for a draught of water. By daylight they were up as usual, and Tommy Rebow, who was out-of-doors the first, came rushing back, singing out—

"Look there! Look there!"

They hurried to the door, expecting to see a vessel; but no sail was in sight. There was, however, in the horizon, a dark cloud, which, though small, was, after they had watched it for some time, evidently increasing in size. On it came, others following, till at length the whole horizon was dark with clouds. Eagerly they rushed forth to put out everything which could hold water, and then rolled up their casks to the side of the tank which they had formed. The whole sky, in the mean time, was overcast with dark clouds.

"There it is! There it is!" cried Jack, pointing to the sea, on which the rain was now pouring down.

On it came, like a wall of water. In a few minutes they were all soaked to the skin, while they lifted up their open mouths to catch the refreshing liquid. Several sails had been washed on shore, and one of these Grimshaw had employed himself in mending. He now brought it up with him, and, calling to his companions, they held it out with one side over one of the casks. So furiously did the rain fall, that the cask was quickly filled. This was indeed providential, for, in spite of all the labour that had been bestowed on the tank, the ground was so sandy that the greater portion of the water ran through it. As soon, however, as the rain had ceased, all hands ran and began to bale out a small quantity which had collected at the bottom. They saved enough to fill about half a cask.

"We should have been badly off, lads, if it had not been for my notion," exclaimed Grimshaw, triumphantly. "My sail has done more than your tank."

"Very true," answered Jack; "but suppose another time the rain was to come in the night, when we were all asleep? The tank would get more than the sail. I have a notion, too, now the ground has been wetted, that if another shower comes the tank will fill better."

With the precious fluid they had collected they returned to the hut, their strength greatly restored from the water they had drunk.

Now, for the first time, Mr Collinson learned to what a fearful state they had been reduced, and felt very grateful to them for the way in which they had supplied him, when they so much wanted the water themselves. Mr Collinson continued very ill; and often Bill, as he sat up watching him, thought that he was going to die.

Rain now frequently fell, and the heat became even greater, at times, than during the bright weather. At length the rain ceased, and the water which had been collected began once more to diminish with fearful rapidity. A long, dry season was before them, and by what means the casks were to be replenished no one could tell.

Chapter Twelve

One night they were all asleep in their hut—for, as there were neither natives nor animals to be feared, no watch was kept—when suddenly Bill was awoke by a loud roaring sound. He could hear the trees above the hut shaking and rustling as if their heads were knocking together, the wind whistling among their boughs. All hands were quickly awake. A hurricane had just broken, and appeared to be far more furious than that when the schooner was wrecked.

"I am afraid the trees will be coming down and crushing us," cried old Grim, starting up.

"It won't do to take Mr Collinson out now," said Bill; "so, if you are afraid of their coming down, I'll stay by him."

Grim went to the door, followed by Jack and Tommy. As they looked out they could see the whole sea, which had been calm as a mirror when they went to sleep, now tossed into high waves topped by foam, which came roaring against the island. Sometimes, indeed, it seemed as if they would roll over it, and sweep them and the hut and everything away, for the reef at the side from which the wind was blowing at that time afforded but slight shelter.

"Look out, lads; we had better say our prayers, for to my mind our last days have come," said old Grim, coming back into the hut.

"I'll say my prayers," said Bill, "whether or not the last day is likely to have come."

"Right, boy," said Mr Collinson, who overheard him. "If all prayed as you do, lad, in times of safety, no one need have cause to tremble in danger. However, lads, you need not fear that the sea will break over the island. Depend upon it, this hurricane is not worse than has often blown in these latitudes; and if the sea had ever broken over the island, these tall trees would not be standing. There is no fear either, I think, of their coming down. Our hut, too, seems to stand securely, thanks to your carpentering, and the strong way in which it has been built. Very likely many a larger mansion will be unroofed to-night by the wind which spares our little hut."

Encouraged by Mr Collinson, his companions again lay down, but of course to sleep was impossible. They, therefore, passed the remainder of the night in conversation, though they had to raise their voices to make themselves heard. The more furious hurricanes often do not last for any length of time. By the time the sun once more rose, the wind had abated, and rapidly falling, there was once more a calm. Bill was the first to go out of the hut, for the rest of the party, as the noise ceased, had gradually fallen off to sleep again. As he looked seaward, his eyes caught sight of a dark object floating at some distance from the land. A second glance only was required to show him that it was a dismasted vessel. With the hope that she might perhaps afford them the means of escaping, he hurried back with the Intelligence into the hut. The whole party, with the exception of the lieutenant, were quickly on their feet, rushing out to see the stranger. Mr Collinson, hearing their exclamations, in spite of his weakness, rose from his bed and followed them.

"I should not mind going out on the raft, if either of you will accompany me," cried Jack Windy. "It's a long pull, to be sure; but if we don't get quickly on board she may be drifting by, and be still farther off than she is now."

"My lads," said Mr Collinson, "I should not like to separate. I would therefore rather increase the size of our fishing-raft, and all go off together. Those on board will be glad of your assistance, probably; and, considering that our provisions and water have nearly come to an end, we cannot be worse off than we shall be in the course of a few days. I believe God in His mercy has sent that vessel to our assistance. Had she not been dismasted, she would have passed by, and we could not have got aboard of her."

The lieutenant's proposal pleased all hands. They immediately set to work to increase the size of their raft, by placing some broken spars on either side, which projected a considerable distance fore and aft, and lashing spars across them. A couple of fresh paddles were also made, and a larger one to serve as a rudder. The sail already used was sufficient in case a breeze should favour them. While they were employed, they constantly looked up to the vessel to see if she was drifting away, but she seemed rather to get nearer than farther off. So eager had they been, that no one had thought of breakfast. Mr Collinson, however, insisted that they should take a good meal before starting.

"We do not know how long it may be before we shall reach the vessel, and, at all events, it will be pretty hard work," he observed.

By his directions, also, the cask containing the remaining stock of water was placed in the centre of the raft, and lashed there securely. Two other casks were placed below the raft to give it greater buoyancy. As soon as all was ready, Mr Collinson was lifted on to the raft, for he was as yet too weak to walk. A seat had been formed for him where he could sit and steer. Jack and old Grim paddled in the forepart of the raft, while Bill and Tommy stood, or rather knelt, farther astern. A couple of poles had been provided, with which the two men shoved off the raft, and then, when they were in deep water, all hands began to paddle away with might and main. It was satisfactory to find that they could go ahead faster than they had expected. They now began to speculate what sort of vessel was the one in sight. They judged her to be of no great size—a brig, or barque, perhaps; a trader, at all events; but whether English, American, French, or Spanish, it was hard to say at that distance. Unaccustomed of late to much exercise, they found the work very hard. The sun, too, came down from the blue sky with intense heat upon their heads. Fortunately they had protected them with caps, or turbans rather, made out of bits of sail-cloth, their own hats having been lost when they were washed ashore. They now also felt grateful to Mr Collinson for having advised them to bring a good supply of water, and over and over again they dipped their tin mug into it, to satisfy the burning thirst which the heat produced.

"I wonder if they see us coming," said Bill. "I should think, by this time, they would have caught sight of the raft."

"Maybe they have plenty to do to look after themselves," said Jack, "working away to get up jury-masts, and labouring at the pumps. Depend upon it, when we get on board we shall not have an idle life of it."

"If foreigners, they will make us work like galley-slaves, I have a notion," observed old Grim. "I think, after all, it would have been better if we had stayed where we were."

Mr Collinson, who had discovered Grimshaw's character by this time, made no remark, but let him talk on. It seemed to those paddling the raft that the longer they paddled the farther off was the vessel. Still, urged by their officer, they persevered. They now began to scan her more narrowly, but still could not determine of what nation she was.

"We hope, lads, that they will prove friends," said Mr Collinson, "and at all events when they hear our story, unless they are brutes indeed, they can scarcely fail to treat us kindly."

"Not so sure of that," growled out old Grim. "They won't eat us, maybe, but if they take us on board, it will be to work for them; we may depend on that."

Such remarks, made occasionally, assisted to pass the time. At length they really were convinced that they had got very much nearer the vessel. Still no one could be seen on board. There she lay, floating quietly on the calm sea, and, except that her masts were gone, not having apparently suffered much in the hurricane. On and on they paddled. At length, having got within hailing distance of the vessel, which they now discovered was certainly a brig, Jack shouted out—

"Brig, ahoy!"

No answer came in return. They drew nearer and nearer. Again he shouted, but without receiving a reply. It now became nearly certain that no one was on board. At length they got alongside, and Jack made fast the raft by a rope which was hanging over the main-chains. By the same means he hauled himself up. As he reached the deck, he gazed around. No one was to be seen.

"We have the ship to ourselves, sir," he said, looking over the side. "Will you come up?"

"Of course," said Mr Collinson.

However, he found it impossible to do so by himself. The two boys, therefore, sprung into the chains, and old Grim remained on the raft to assist him up. It was not without difficulty that he at length got on board. The brig had suffered more than they had at first supposed in the hurricane. Her bulwarks on the opposite side had been completely stove in, her boats had been carried away and her deck swept of everything. Altogether, she was in a deplorable condition. Still, as some of the rigging remained attached to her, and there were probably spare spars below, Mr Collinson told the men that he proposed getting up jury-masts, and endeavouring to carry the vessel to Port Royal.

"It may be a long business, though," he observed; "and first, lads, get up our cask of water. That is the most precious thing out here, and we must not throw a drop away. Very likely we shall not find an over-supply on board."

He spoke just in time, for Tommy, fancying that the raft would no longer be wanted, was on the point of letting it go.

"Hold fast with the raft too," said the lieutenant. "As we have no boat, it is possible we may yet find it of use."

The cask having been hoisted up, with a few other articles which had been brought off, as well as the paddles and mast, the raft was veered astern.

"As we are afloat again, lads, I must once more take the command," said Mr Collinson. "Jack Windy, do you and Bill Sunnyside go below, and come and report to me what you see. Grimshaw, sound the well. After the battering the brig must have had, she must be making a good deal of water."

Old Grim soon returned aft, reporting that there was six feet of water in the hold.

"That looks bad," observed the lieutenant. "However, some may have got in when the sea which carried away the masts struck the vessel."

While he was speaking Jack and Bill came hurrying up from below.

"Oh! Sir," exclaimed Jack, "I don't like the look of things at all. We have found two people in the cabin—dead—who, from their looks, I am pretty certain, died of yellow fever; if so, it will be a bad job for us."

"It may be so," said Mr Collinson. "At all events, we shall be wise then not to live below. Go forward, and see if there are any people there. Bill, do you stay on deck."

Jack disappeared down the fore-hatchway, but directly afterwards returned with a look of horror.

"There are three poor fellows there, sir. One of them is alive; but, from the way he was crying out, I don't think he can live many minutes longer. She looks to me like a French vessel—at all events, she is not English."

This announcement was truly alarming. Mr Collinson told the men to carry him down, that he might see the poor sick man.

"We don't want to be mutinous, sir," answered Jack, "but that is what we won't do. You are ill already, and more likely to catch the fever than we are. I'll carry him down a mug of water, maybe that will do him good, but it's little use any of us can be to him, I have a notion."

Saying this, Jack again disappeared down the fore-hatch. He quickly returned.

"It was of no use, sir," he said. "No sooner did I put the water to the poor fellow's lips, than he gave a gasp and off he went. And now, sir, there are five of them lying there all dead. The sooner we get them up and overboard the better."

Mr Collinson agreed to this, and the two men accordingly went at once into the cabin, and returned bringing a man, whom from his appearance they supposed to have been the captain. Without more ado, they slid the body overboard. Thus one after the other was treated. There was no time for ceremony of any sort. For their own safety, the great point was to get rid of the bodies at once. A tar-pot having been found, Mr Collinson then sent the men below, to fumigate the cabin and the forepeak.

"If we do that thoroughly, I trust that we need not fear the fever," he observed. "At all events, let us put our faith in Providence, and pray that we may be preserved."

Chapter Thirteen

There was no time for any one to be idle on board the brig. She had received a tremendous shaking in the hurricane, and was leaking considerably. It was a wonder, indeed, that she had not gone down. To have a chance of safety, jury-masts must be got up before another breeze should come on, or she might be driven on the reefs and lost.

Jack, having searched the cabin, brought all the papers he could find to Mr Collinson. By this he discovered that the brig was the *Beatrix*, bound from New Orleans to Point à Petre in Dominique.

"Poor fellows! Some probably died from the yellow fever before the hurricane came on, and the rest, unable to shorten sail in time, must have been washed overboard when the masts were carried away, as the wind struck her," observed Mr Collinson. "Pray Heaven that we may be preserved; but I will not deceive you, lads; it will require all your courage and resolution to carry the vessel safely into port. We have a long passage before us, and I will do my best to navigate her, but I can do little more."

"And we will do our best, Mr Collinson, to obey your orders," answered Jack Windy.

"Then, Jack, the first thing will be to get hold of a quadrant and chart, and navigation books. Without these it will be very guess-work. Fortunately, I understand the French; so that, if they are found, there will not be much difficulty in the matter."

As soon as Bill heard this, he hurried below, and soon returned with several books, a chart, and a quadrant.

"The first thing is to know whereabouts we are," said the lieutenant; "and, as it must be nearly noon, I will take an observation at once. You must lift me up, though, lads; I am too weak to stand."

Supported by Jack and Bill Sunnyside, the lieutenant leant against the companion-hatch, and made the required observation.

"I was only just in time, though," he remarked. "The sun dipped not two minutes after I got a sight of him through the instrument. There," he said, pointing to a spot on the chart, "is where, by my calculations, we now are. If you steer south-west, you will make Cape Saint Antonio, at the westernmost end of Cuba; but look out for the Colorados, and do not run the ship upon them. I tell you this, should anything happen to me."

"But we hope, sir, nothing will happen to you," said Jack, "and that you will live to carry in the brig to Port Royal, before many weeks are over."

Mr Collinson replied that he had little hopes himself of ever again seeing land.

There appeared to be no want of provisions on board, for even in the cabin a couple of hams and cheese and a cask of biscuit were found, with several other articles; and on deck was a water-butt, which, having been tightly bunged and well secured, had escaped being washed away, or filled with salt water.

All hands now set to work to get up spars from below, and canvas, and rope. As the wind came from the northward, they were eager to make sail without loss of time. Spars were therefore secured to the stumps of the masts, and stayed up, and a couple of royals set on them. Fortunately, the rudder had escaped injury; and though, as Jack Windy observed, the brig was under-rigged, she slipped through the water at the rate of a couple of miles an hour.

"'It's a long lane that has no turning,' I've heard say," said Bill; "and it's a long voyage, I conclude, that has no ending; and so, I suppose, if the brig keeps afloat as long, we shall reach port at last."

"You may well say '*if,*'" observed old Grim; "but, to my mind, the water's coming in faster than we are likely to pump it out; and directly we get a bit of a sea on, it will play old Harry with us."

Though old Grim grumbled on all occasions, yet he worked as hard as anybody else, and so nobody minded his grumbling. The very worst sort of character is the fellow who grumbles and does not work; and there are some such on board ships, as well as on shore.

Having got up their temporary masts, they now set to work to build more permanent ones. In this, old Grim showed a good deal of skill, and ably carried out Mr Collinson's directions. Darkness put an end to their labours. They, in the mean time, however, had rigged an awning on deck, under which Mr Collinson might sleep, for they agreed that it might not be wise to remain any length of time in the cabin. Jack and Bill took one watch, and old Grim and Tommy Rebow the other.

The binnacle as well as the wheel had escaped, and, oil being found, they were able to light the lamp at night. Bill had already learned to take his trick at the helm. He was therefore able to steer part of his time during his watch; indeed, there was no great difficulty, in consequence of the small amount of sail the brig was carrying. When Jack came aft to take the helm, Bill remembered what old Grim had said.

"Don't you think it will be as well for us to try to sound the well, and see if the vessel has made more water?" he asked.

"Yes; hold on for a minute, and I will do it," said Jack.

He came aft again in a short time.

"To my mind, she's leaking faster than is pleasant," he observed. "If you will stand to the helm, I will rig the pump, and see if we can't clear her a little."

In a short time the pump was heard going. It awoke Mr Collinson.

"I thought it would be safer, sir, to keep the pump going," sung out Jack; "but don't be concerned about it, sir; it's just on the safe side."

Jack pumped and pumped away till he could pump no longer; he then went and roused up old Grim, who grumbled fearfully.

"Come, Grimshaw," he said, "just you take a spell at the pump. If we cannot manage to stop the leak, or to get the vessel clear, there's not much chance of our getting into Port Royal harbour, that I can see."

Old Grim, although he grumbled, pumped away as lustily as Jack; and then Tommy jumped up and took a spell, and when he was tired he called Bill, and took his place at the helm; and thus they went on till daylight, when Grim declared the water was considerably lessened in the hold. This gave them encouragement. Poor Mr Collinson felt very much vexed that he could not help. The men would not hear of it.

"No, sir, you just lie quiet there. Our lives depend upon your holding on, as much as your life depends on our exertions; for if you were to leave us, how should we ever find our way into port again?"

Jack insisted that the two boys should lie down again, and get some rest, while he and Grimshaw took it by turns at the pump. At length they agreed that by labouring at the pump every alternate hour, they might keep the leak under. They now again turned to, to get up jury-masts. A sufficient supply of rope was found for the standing rigging, and by night they had a very respectable foremast stepped and well secured with a short jib-boom, on which a fore-staysail was set. The night was spent much as the former had been, though all hands began to feel very weary with their exertions. Their only comfort was that Mr Collinson appeared to be gaining strength. Although the caboose had been carried away, there was a stove in the cabin, and in this they were able to cook their provisions. Some good tea was found, and other luxuries, which tended much to restore the lieutenant's health. The following day they got up a mainmast, and besides this they rigged a small mizzen-mast, on which they were able to set a sail to assist in steering the vessel. It was rigged just in time, for the wind began to draw somewhat round to the north-west, making the coast of Cuba, which at length appeared in sight, a lee shore. They hauled up, therefore; but not without some anxiety weathered the Colorados, which they saw not a couple of miles to leeward of them.

In a short time, Mr Collinson was well enough to take the helm for several hours each day, giving more time to his small crew to work the pump and obtain necessary rest. At length Cape Saint Antonio appeared in sight; and, weathering it, the course was altered to south-east. Once more they were out of sight of land. Mr Collinson had showed all of them the chart, that they might the better understand where they were going, and that the progress they had made might keep up their spirits. They had still a passage of some four or five hundred miles before them; but though their vessel was somewhat leaky, and even with a good breeze they could not make more than three or four knots an hour, still, as Bill observed, "it must some day or other come to an end."

The brig was now about mid-way between the main land of Central America and Cuba, when the wind, which had been for some time light, dropped altogether. In vain old Grim growled; in vain Jack whistled for a breeze. The water they had brought on board, as well as that in the cask, was almost exhausted.

"It will be pretty well time to be getting this cask filled again," observed old Grim, as he drew out a tin cupful of water. "I will just go down below, and see about getting up another."

He was a considerable time absent, hunting about with a lantern in his hand. At length he came up again, with a look of dismay on his countenance.

"Jack," he said, "do you know I have been hunting from stem to stern, and not a cask, which looks as if it had water in it, can I find?"

Mr Collinson, who was steering at the time, guessed from the looks of the men that something was wrong.

"We ought to have economised it more," he observed; "it was wrong in me not to warn you. However, we must make the most of what we have got; and perhaps in another search we may be more fortunate."

"I will have a look," said Jack; "and here, Bill, you come with me."

Jack and Bill hunted about as old Grim had done. At length, he appeared under the hatchway, and shouted out—

"Here's a cask of some sort, at all events: it contains liquor, if it does not contain water."

The cask was got up.

"You must promise me, lads, if that cask contains spirits, not to drink it. Let's broach it, however, and see."

On a hole being bored, wine spouted out.

"We should be thankful for this," said Mr Collinson, "it is light claret, and a small quantity will probably do us all good."

It was arranged that a pint of wine only should be taken by each of them every day. This would save the consumption of water.

"I would rather it had been water," said old Grim; "though, to be sure, the wine is not bad, and I should not mind if it had been a little stronger."

The calm continued. The sea was like glass. Chips of wood, even some feathers, thrown overboard, did not move from the side of the vessel. There she lay, her battered sides reflected in the mirror-like surface of the ocean. Now her head slowly moved round in one direction, now in another, but no progress was made. At night they lay down, hoping that the morning would bring a breeze; but when the morning sun began its upward course, his rays getting hotter and hotter, till the pitch in the seams bubbled and hissed, on he went, passing almost overhead, till he again glided down into his ocean bed in the west.

Chapter Fourteen

Day after day, the brig floated on the motionless ocean. The water was almost exhausted, so also was the cask of claret. There was still some food remaining, but, without water, it would be of little avail in keeping those on board the brig alive. Grimshaw had hitherto kept up his spirits, as well as the rest of the party, but he and Tommy Rebow declared that they would work no more, that the vessel was doomed to destruction, and that sink she would in the course of a few days.

"But before that time, perhaps, a breeze will spring up, and we shall be slipping along merrily through the water," observed Sunshine Bill.

"We shall be slipping down to the bottom, rather," said Old Grim. "Though we have been pumping away till we have nearly pumped our arms off, the water has been gaining upon us for the last two days, to my knowledge. It comes in all round the vessel, and human power can no longer keep her afloat."

Even Mr Collinson looked graver than he had done for some time. He was now able to take an occasional spell at the pumps, and, as if to shame Grimshaw, he took hold of the brake. After working away for some time, he sounded the well His countenance showed that there was more water in the vessel than he liked.

"My lads," he said at length, "I am afraid, after all, that we shall be unable to keep the brig afloat. At all events, in case she should go down, it will be wise to have some means of saving our lives. Our raft is small for a long voyage: we will, therefore, haul it up alongside, and enlarge and strengthen it. It will enable us to keep afloat till some vessel passes, though I cannot promise you that we should be able to reach Jamaica on it."

Several empty bottles had been found in the cabin, and into these all the water that remained was put, as was also the claret into others. They, with the remainder of the biscuit and meat which had been found, were put ready to place on the raft. In the mean time, following Mr Collinson's directions, they increased and strengthened the raft. This being done, it was once more dropped astern. The heat and the anxiety they underwent was now telling on all hands. Mr Collinson again became ill; indeed, none of the party were in a much better condition. Still they had to keep their watch at night as usual. Bill was forward, looking out over the ocean, and wishing that a breeze would come, when he cried out—

"See! See! She's coming towards us! I see her white canvas shining in the moonlight. She's coming on fast. Look, Jack, look! Can't you make her out?"

Jack Windy at first declared he could see nothing, but when Bill more clearly described the vessel, he also asserted that he saw her. Yet not a breath of wind had reached them. On came the stranger.

"Shall we call up Mr Collinson?" asked Bill.

"No, no, boy, I can't make it out. Don't say anything. I fancied I heard a voice hail us; yet I don't know. Why, there she goes, not two cables' length off from us. I could almost declare I saw the people on her deck. Yet I have never before seen a vessel sailing head to wind, as some say they do, or in a calm like this."

Rapidly the vessel glided away to the east, till she was lost to sight.

"Boy, this is the strangest thing I ever saw in my life," said Jack Windy. "It's not a thing I should like to talk about—no more will you, I have a notion—yet both of us saw it, I'll swear to that."

On calling Grimshaw and Tommy to relieve the deck, they could not resist telling them what they had seen.

"Maybe we shall see something of the same sort," said old Grim. "I don't like those sort of things, but I am not surprised."

When daylight broke, old Grim declared that he also had seen a vessel passing rapidly by, and disappearing to the east. They determined to tell Mr Collinson.

"I am not surprised," he answered, "at what you tell me, my lads; but I have to assure you that the vessels you think you have seen have been all the time inside your own brains. Bill thought he saw a vessel, and that made Jack think he had seen one; and when they told Grimshaw and Tommy Rebow, it made them fancy the same; but, depend upon it, you have not, in reality, seen a vessel of any sort. If God should wish to relieve us, He will send one in His own good time; but if not, He has His reasons for leaving us alone."

"That I am sure He will have, sir," said Bill.

They waited the whole of the day, anxiously looking out for the sight of a breeze, but still round them was the same unbroken surface of water, blue and shining in the day, and dark and leaden at night. The water in their cask was decreasing fearfully; their provisions, also, were nearly exhausted. Though they kept lines overboard, and Bill was constantly fishing, no fish were caught. At last they gave up even attempting to catch them. As their strength decreased from want of food and water, they were less able to work the pump. The consequence was, the leak again gained upon them. All but Bill began to despair. He, true to his principles, kept up his spirits.

"Well, Bill, I do envy you," said Tommy Rebow; "but your hoping is of no use. If the vessel does not go down, we shall all be starved in a few days, so it will make but little difference."

"I don't say that," said Bill. "A breeze will some day or other spring up, and then, in this narrow sea, some vessel must surely pass us, and it's not likely that they would leave us to perish; and if not, we may still be able to carry the vessel to some land or other, even if we can't carry her to Jamaica, where we shall find provisions and water. I think it's wrong, therefore, to despair. Let's trust in God. He has taken care of us up to this time, do not you think He can take care of us still longer? He can't be tired of looking after us, and if He cared for us once, He will care for us still."

Still neither Tom nor the rest of the party could recover their spirits. At length one night it was Jack and Bill's watch. Jack had sat down and dropped off to sleep, for he had little strength remaining, and all his spirits were gone. Bill, however, kept awake. He was standing at the helm, for though there was no wind, the sails were set ready to catch the first breath of air which might come to them. As he was looking round, he thought he saw a dark line on the water. It rapidly approached.

"Jack! Jack!" he shouted out, "here comes the breeze!"

But poor Jack was fast asleep, and fancied when he heard Bill's voice that he was only dreaming. Again Bill shouted. The vessel began to lift with the heaving sea. Jack sprang to his feet.

"A breeze! A breeze!" he shouted out, running to the sheets; but at that instant a strong blast struck the vessel, and before the rest of the crew could come on deck, with a loud crash both the masts were carried away, and the brig lay as helpless as at first on the water.

With great exertions, however, the spars and sails were saved, and got inboard. Still, it was evident that nothing could be done that night, and they must wait till the wind abated, before they could again get up their masts and sails.

"We have been waiting for this breeze, lads," said Mr Collinson, "and now it has come, we ought to make the best use we can of it. Even if we can rig a rag of a sail forward, it will help us along."

Though weak and ill, Mr Collinson set the example, and at length a short spar with a royal was fixed to the stump of the foremast. Aided by this, the vessel ran on before the wind. The breeze, however, though moderate at first, increased towards daylight, and the vessel now began to pitch and roll greatly. In the morning, when old Grim, who acted as cook, sent Tommy for some water, he returned with a look of dismay. Not a drop remained in the cask. This was sad news.

"Give me a lantern," said Bill; "and, Tommy, you and I will have another hunt, and see if there is another cask to be found."

"It's of no use," observed old Grim; "I hunted everywhere, and could not find one."

"Maybe we shall be more fortunate," said Bill; and, taking the lantern, he and Tommy went down into the hold. The water was washing about fearfully inside, and he could not help fearing that a good deal more was now coming in than during the calm. There was some danger, too, of their being struck by various articles which were tumbling about in the hold, having broken loose, or been washed up by the water.

"See! See!" cried Bill. "Hold up the lantern! Why, that looks like a water-cask!"

They waited till the vessel seemed steady for a moment; then, making a rush together, they caught hold of the cask. It was but a small one, such as was used to bring the water off, in boats, from the shore. It was full: there was no doubt about that. Having secured it under the hatchway, Bill told Tommy to go and call Jack or old Grim to assist them in getting it up. Jack soon came down with a tackle, and the cask was hoisted up on deck. It was quickly opened. Mr Collinson praised Bill very much for finding it.

"And now, lads," he said, "we must consider this worth its weight in gold, and more than that, too."

The men promised to husband it with the greatest care. All hands now went below, to search for more provisions, while Mr Collinson remained at the helm. A few onions were discovered, and another small cask of biscuits, but they were somewhat damaged by the salt water. Nothing else eatable could be found. Even during the short time they had been below, the wind had increased considerably, and the vessel was now tumbling about more than ever. Jack's face, too, looked unusually long as he went up to Mr Collinson.

"I am afraid, sir, the brig won't swim many hours longer, for, as she rolls about, the water comes pouring in on both sides."

"I was afraid it would be so," said Mr Collinson. "We must have another spell at the pumps, then."

"Very little use in that, sir," said old Grim. "I don't think if we were to pump spell after spell we should keep the vessel afloat. To my mind, if there's any shore near, we should steer directly for it, and even then I doubt if we should reach it."

Under the present circumstances, Grim could venture to speak to an officer with more freedom than on ordinary occasions. Although Mr Collinson wished to keep up the men's spirits, he could not help seeing that they were right. Indeed, from the peculiar motion of the vessel, in a short time he began to fear that she would not float even as long as they had expected. All this time the raft had been towing astern. It was well-built, or it would have come to pieces from the tossing about it was now receiving. Should the vessel go down, it was their only hope. Still the lieutenant determined to try and save her; and, going to the pump, he began working away himself. Jack followed him, and even old Grim took a spell. He worked on for some time.

"It's of no use," he said at length; "I am sure we are not keeping the water under."

It was too evident that he was right, as it came in faster than ever. Mr Collinson now ordered them to bring the water-cask, and their scanty supply of provisions, and a few other articles up on deck, ready to lower down on the raft.

Chapter Fifteen

Although the water was rushing into the vessel with a rapidity which gave no hope of her floating much longer, the wind was at the same time going down. There was thus some prospect of their lives being preserved, uncertain though they felt it must be. Every now and then, either Jack or Grimshaw went below to ascertain the progress the water was making. At length Grim came hurrying up.

"No time to lose, sir; I am very sure of that!" he shouted out. "If we don't look sharp, the brig will be sinking under us!"

"Haul up the raft, then," said Mr Collinson. "The boys must go first on it."

It was hauled up under the stern, and Bill and Tommy lowered themselves down; Grimshaw followed, and Mr Collinson and Jack then lowered down the various articles they had collected to take with them, which Grim and the boys secured as well as they could. Mr Collinson told Jack to descend, and, casting an eye round, he saw that nothing was left behind. He himself then slid down upon the raft, and was caught by his companions. He had scarcely calculated how weak he was; and, had it not been for the men, he would have fallen into the water. His eye had been on the stern of the vessel. He saw it give a peculiar movement, lifting upwards.

"Cut! Cut!" he shouted.

Jack was just in time to cut the tow-rope, and with a long pole to shove off, before, the vessel's stern lifting high in the air, she went down bows foremost. Then, getting out the paddles, they paddled away quickly to avoid being drawn down in the vortex.

"Well, we are unlucky!" cried old Grim, as he saw the vessel go down.

"I think rather we are very fortunate," said Bill. "Suppose we had not had the raft, where should we be now? We ought to thank Him who has preserved us, and not to cry out that we are unlucky."

Bill had always some answer to make to old Grim's growls.

"You are right, boy," said Mr Collinson. "I calculate that we are not more than fifty miles from the American coast, if so much; and if the wind comes from the north, as I think it is likely to do, we shall be able to reach it in a couple of days or so: besides which, we are nearly certain to fall in with some vessel before long, even if we cannot reach the shore."

Though the lieutenant made these remarks, he could not help confessing to himself that there were still many dangers to be encountered. The wind having gone down sufficiently, they were able to hoist their sail, and to steer towards the nearest point of the American coast, which lay about south-west from them.

The lieutenant felt their condition even more than his companions. He had been indulging in the hope of sighting Jamaica in the course of a few days: and now he could not tell when he might get back to that island. He calculated, too, that the *Lilly* would have returned there, and that his friends would have become very anxious at not seeing him. He felt far more for Ellen Lydall than for himself.

For some time the raft glided on, but the wind was gradually falling, and before the sun went down there was again a perfect calm. Although it could be urged on by paddles, yet, weak and fatigued as all hands were, but slow progress could be made in that way, while neither water nor provisions would hold out till they could reach the land. The sea went down with the wind, and the raft became now perfectly tranquil, enabling those on it to go to sleep without fear of being washed off. One at a time only remained awake to keep watch, though there was not much object in doing so, as, during the calm, no vessel could come near them. At length the sun again rose and glided through the blue sky, in which not a cloud appeared to give indication of a change of weather. His rays beat down on the heads of the seamen on the raft, making them long for a shady place.

Hour after hour the calm continued, and there they floated in the centre, as it were, of a vast mirror, covered by a blue canopy. Very little was said now by any of the party. Even Bill could scarcely sing a verse of a song, though he made several attempts, to keep up his own spirits and those of his companions. Hour after hour passed by; the night again came. Often, during the period of darkness, those on the raft thought they saw vessels approaching, but as they drew near they vanished into thin air. Sometimes, too, they declared they heard voices shouting to them. Even Mr Collinson could scarcely persuade himself, at times, when he heard his companions talking of the vessels drawing near, that he did not also see them. They seldom moved, except to hand the cup of precious water round one to the other, that they might moisten their lips. Oh, how precious that water was now becoming!

The last drop was at length exhausted, and for some time they had not taken sufficient to quench their thirst. That thirst increased till it became almost intolerable. What would they not have given for one single bottle-full? Mr Collinson charged them on no account to be tempted to drink the salt water.

"Madness and death will be the consequence, if you do," he observed.

Still, with difficulty they could refrain from taking the tempting fluid on which they floated. As morning approached, Bill, who was standing up, declared that he felt a light breeze on his cheeks. It lasted for a short time again. Then again it came, and, as the sun rose, it could be seen playing, here and there, over the water.

"And see! See! There comes a sail!" cried Jack.

He pointed to the westward. There, just rising above the horizon, were seen the topgallant sails of a ship. How eagerly did they watch her! She was standing towards them; there was no doubt about that. On she came, but the wind was light, and she advanced but slowly. They had but a few damaged biscuits and onions remaining. Should she not perceive them, starvation might be their fate. The time went by. It had never appeared to pass so slowly. Still she was getting nearer. Her topsails gradually rose above the water; then her courses were seen; and, finally, the hull itself rose in sight.

During this time, the sun was rising in the heavens, and struck down upon their heads with terrific fury, increasing the fearful thirst from which they were suffering. It increased their longing for her approach. She seemed to come on very, very slowly; indeed, sometimes they felt as if they could scarcely hold out till she could get up to them.

"I don't think, after all, she will pass near enough to see us," observed old Grim.

They watched her again for some time.

"Yes! Yes! She's altering her course. She is steering directly for us now!" exclaimed Jack. "We're seen! We're seen!" he and Bill shouted in chorus.

Mr Collinson had made no remark. He had been examining the vessel, and felt sure, from her appearance, that she was French. She was a flush-deck vessel, probably a privateer. Still their lives might be preserved, as those on board would scarcely have the barbarity to refuse to receive them. He said nothing, however, to his companions.

On came the vessel. As she approached, her topsails were clewed up, and a boat was lowered. The boat approached. Their wretched appearance, suffering from burning thirst and hunger, might have excited the compassion of even the most hardhearted. The people in the boat shouted to them.

"They're Frenchmen!" cried old Grim. "They're somewhat better than Spaniards, that's all I can say in their favour!"

As the boat drew near, the party on the raft pointed to their lips.

"Water! Water!" they gasped out.

By this time, no one could speak with clearness. Even Jack Windy, who was the strongest, could scarcely stand upright on the raft.

"Oh! Pauvres garçons! Vîte! Vîte!"

Mr Collinson understood the words. It showed him that the men in the boat could feel for their sufferings. They were soon lifted into it, with the few articles which they had brought with them, and the boat then quickly pulled towards the ship. They were hoisted on board, for they could not help themselves. Mr Collinson was allowed to rest on a gun-carriage, near the gangway, while the rest of the party were left standing or leaning against the bulwarks. Bill and Tommy sunk down from weakness on the deck. The French seamen, however, immediately brought them up a jug of water, of which they eagerly drank.

"Well, this is sweet and nice!" said Bill, as he took the cup from his mouth.

The water, though not over-cool, greatly revived them all; and the Frenchmen stood by smiling, till they had emptied the contents of the jug. At length, a tall, stout man, with a very dark complexion, but who, by the uniform he wore, appeared to be an officer, came up to them.

"Who are you?" he demanded in a somewhat rough voice. "But I need not ask that: I see, by your dress, that you are of the English marine. But where did you come from? How did you get on the raft?"

Mr Collinson briefly replied that they had been wrecked, and finding a brig which had been deserted by her crew, they had got on board her; but she had afterwards sunk, leaving them floating on the raft.

"What vessel was she?—Oh yes, I understand," observed the officer; and then, turning to the men, he asked, "To what ship do you belong?"

"The *Lilly*, sir," said Jack, without hesitation.

"The *Lilly*? Why, that's the corvette we fell in with last week, away to the westward. You said she was wrecked," he added, turning to Mr Collinson, and speaking in somewhat broken English, though sufficiently clear to make his meaning understood.

"I said that we were wrecked," replied Mr Collinson. "I did not say that our own ship was wrecked."

"In what vessel, then, were you cast away?" asked the officer.

"In a prize we had taken," answered Mr Collinson. "We were ordered to bring her round to Jamaica; but, being caught in a hurricane, we were driven on a reef in the neighbourhood of the Tortugas."

"I thought so!" exclaimed the officer, with an oath. "She was our consort. You would have had a harder matter to take us, let me tell you. However, it's a satisfaction to find that you lost her. We heard that she was captured. However, it's a good reason why we should treat you as prisoners;—as such you must consider yourselves."

"We must submit, if so you determine it," said Mr Collinson; "but our case is a hard one."

"Not harder than that of the poor fellows who lost their vessel, and are now in one of your prisons in Jamaica."

With this remark, the mulatto officer returned to his companions, to whom he seemed to be imparting the information he had obtained. At length another officer came up to Mr Collinson, and addressed him in French.

"I am the surgeon of the ship," he said. "I see that you are ill, and almost worn out; and, although you are an Englishman and an enemy, you must let me prescribe for you. Come down, therefore, into my cabin, where you can obtain some rest, which I see you greatly require."

"I accept your offer gratefully," answered Mr Collinson; "and I must beg also that you will attend to the wants of my companions."

"It is right in you, monsieur, to think of your men," said the surgeon; "and I will gladly do as you wish. I am afraid that both you and they will be subjected to some unpleasant treatment, for we have some terribly rough people on board, both among the officers and forward." He said this in a low voice. "I will, however, do my best for you."

The seamen at length made signs to old Grim, and Jack, and the boys, that they might go down below. Some seamen then spread out four hammocks in the fore part of the ship, and signed to them that they had better lie down and rest themselves—a proposal which they willingly accepted.

"I suppose they will give us some food," said Jack.

"They cannot fancy we can live upon water and air," observed Bill; "so I dare say, by-and-by, they will."

"They seem to carry on things in a rum man-of-war fashion," observed Grimshaw, pointing along the deck.

The larger portion of the crew appeared to be below, and they were all seated about the decks, some with cards, others with dice, so absorbed in their games that they took no notice of the newcomers. Some few were mending their clothes, or manufacturing various articles; but the greater number of those who were not gambling were talking vehemently, "making all sorts of grimaces," as Grim observed; now and then touching the hilts of the long knives they wore in their belts, as if they were about to start up and stick them into each other. Some were laughing, others uttering strange cries; the losers were swearing, and the gainers shouting with glee. On one side, although there was scarcely room for a tall man to stand upright, a fiddler was playing, with several men dancing round him; while another party were collected round a man who was singing, at the top of his voice, a song which seemed to afford his auditors infinite amusement. In spite of the strange Babel of sounds, however, the weary seamen and two boys at length fell back and dropped off asleep.

Chapter Sixteen

The ship by which Mr Collinson and his companions had been rescued was the *Poisson Volant*, a privateer fitted out at Port a Petre, in Dominique. She had had a long run of ill-luck, so the surgeon told him, and this had put her officers in very bad humour. The dark, stout man was her captain, of whom the surgeon seemed to stand greatly in awe.

"He would make no scruple of shooting any one through the head who offends him, and as I have no fancy to be treated in that way, I purpose, if I can once get on shore, to leave the ship."

This was not very pleasant information; but Mr Collinson hoped to be able to escape giving the tyrant any cause of offence. Bill Sunnyside was very hungry, as were his companions, when they fell asleep. He kept dreaming about feasts, and then at length he thought he was once more at home, and that his mother had got a capital supper ready for him, and that she and his brothers and sisters were collected round the table, and he thought that he himself was, somehow or other, kept out of the room. The smell of the sausages, however, came through a chink in the door, and made him feel still more hungry. He could not open the door, and he could not cry out to ask any one to let him in. Still, there they all sat, with the sausages bubbling away on the table, and the kettle hissing on the hearth, and a large loaf of bread and a big pat of butter, all ready, waiting to be eaten. At length he made a run, and resolved to burst open the door, when he heard old Grim sing out, and he found that he had, somehow or other, tumbled over him. His nostrils were at the same time assailed with savoury odours, and he saw men coming from the galley-fire with pans and dishes from which wreaths of steam were ascending. The mess-tables were quickly spread, and the men began their dinners. Bill and his companions watched them for some minutes, and could then stand it no longer, but getting up, they came to the nearest mess-table, pointing to their mouths. The Frenchmen laughed, and then invited them to join them.

"It was the smell of their dinner made me dream," thought Bill, as he thankfully accepted the dish of soup and meat which was handed to him. Never had he eaten a more delicious mess; hunger, indeed, increased its flavour, and he did his best to show the Frenchmen the satisfaction it afforded him. They seemed much amused when he held out his bowl for more. Of course, Bill could not understand what was said, as none appeared to speak English. When dinner was over, Bill and his companions were allowed to lie down again out of the way, on the hammocks, and were once more quickly asleep. They woke up again at supper-time, when Bill felt himself perfectly ready for another meal. The next day, however, the Frenchmen looked somewhat sulkily at them, and some hard biscuit and water was given them for breakfast; while at dinner, instead of being invited to the messes, a bowl of soup was placed before them, from which, by signs, they understood they were to help themselves. The next day their bedding was taken away, and they found that they had only the hard deck to lie upon. Grimshaw, as may be supposed, grumbled greatly.

"We must bear it, however," said Bill. "The voyage will come to an end before long; then, I suppose, if the English have got hold of any Frenchmen, these people will be glad to give us up, and get them back instead. I wonder how Mr Collinson is getting on? I hope they don't treat him as they do us."

Although Grimshaw grumbled, he could not help acknowledging that they were all gaining health and strength, with the rest they were enjoying; and in the course of three days they were so much better, that they could manage to crawl on deck. The wind had been very light, so they had made but little progress. As they were able to get into a shady place, the fresh air revived them. Bill looked aft, anxiously looking for Mr Collinson, but he did not appear. When he attempted to go aft himself, one of the seamen made signs to him that he was to remain where he was. The ship was running some three or four knots only through the water, with all sail set.

"I say, Tommy," said Bill to his companion, "there's another chance of our escaping a French prison. What do you think if the *Lilly*, or some other ship of war, was to fall in with us? That would be a happy thing."

"I don't know," answered Tommy. "Perhaps they would cut our throats and throw us overboard, just in revenge. They look as if they were up to anything of that sort."

"No no, Tommy! Don't be cast down. I would run the risk of that, for, rough as they are, I don't think they would do anything as bad as that."

At length the town of Point a Petre, in the island of Dominique, appeared in sight. All this time they had not seen Mr Collinson, nor had they been able to hear anything about him. When the ship came to an anchor, they were ordered below. After some time they were called on deck, and they then saw that a French boat with six soldiers was alongside.

"You Englishmen, get into that boat!" shouted the mulatto captain.

They of course obeyed. As soon as they were in her, they saw Mr Collinson, who had just then come up on deck, look over the side.

"Glad, sir, to see that no harm has happened to you," shouted Jack. "We hope you are coming with us."

"I believe I am, my men; and thanks to you for your kind wishes," answered Mr Collinson, who just then turned round to shake hands with the surgeon. Directly afterwards, he came down the side into the boat.

As soon as they landed, they were taken up before a military officer, who cross-questioned them, by means of an interpreter, addressing Mr Collinson directly in French.

"You are to be sent into the interior," said the interpreter, "and you will there remain, till the war is concluded."

Their examination being over, they were taken away by the guards who had them in charge. Mr Collinson had, fortunately, his purse in his pocket with a few gold pieces.

"Now, my men," he said, "I wish to lay this out to the best advantage of us all. If I spend it in clothing, which we all very much want, we shall have nothing to buy food. I will, therefore, reserve it for an emergency."

The lieutenant, however, supplied the party with hats, which they very much wanted. Though shoes would have been pleasant, they could still do without them. Their clothes were, as may be supposed, in a sadly tattered condition. To obtain new ones, was out of the question. Their guards, however, allowed them to go to the barber's, where, their hair being cut, they looked a little less like Robinson Crusoes than they had hitherto done. They were then marched to the prison, and were all shut up in a room, with no greater indulgence shown to Mr Collinson than to them.

"It's a great shame!" exclaimed Jack Windy, "to treat our officer in this way. It's all very right and proper for us, but they ought to show more respect, that they ought."

"Never mind, my lad," said Mr Collinson. "I thank you for your good feeling, and more faithful, kind fellows I could not wish to be cast among."

Next day the gaoler came in, and told them they were to prepare for a journey, and in a short time they were brought out of prison, at the door of which they found four mules waiting to carry them, with a guard of black soldiers.

"You speak French?" said a man, addressing the first lieutenant. "Tell your people, then, that each of the men is to mount a mule, while one will serve for the two boys. You take the other."

The animals were far from gaily caparisoned, straw packs on their backs serving the place of saddles. The boys quickly climbed up to the back of their beast, while the lieutenant and the two men mounted theirs.

"Forward!" was the word given, and they moved on, the black soldiers, grinning and gabbling negro French, running by their sides. They were soon out of the town, and proceeding along a dusty road, with coffee-plantations on either side, no trees remaining to shelter them from the sun. At length, however, they got into a wilder part of the country, where the dense tropical vegetation occasionally afforded them shade. After some miles, they came in sight of a large country house. Hot, thirsty, and weary, they turned their eyes towards it, wishing that some of the inmates might have the charity to invite them to stop and rest.

"If you will tell me what to say, sir, I will go and ask," said Bill, "if the guards will let me."

Mr Collinson advised him simply to point to his mouth, and to make signs that he was very weary. The guards, who were entertaining, perhaps, the same ideas as their prisoners, without difficulty let Bill go off, while they drew up in the shade near the house. In a short time Bill returned.

"It's all right, sir," he said. "There was a tall young lady came out, and she looked so kindly at me when I spoke; and when I pointed to you all here, she made signs that we were to come up to the house."

Mr Collinson, on this, explained to the guards what the boy said, and the whole party proceeded to the wide steps which led up to the entrance-door, under a deep verandah. The young lady was there. Mr Collinson took off his hat, and explained in his best French who they were.

"Oh!" she said, "my father will be at home presently, and he, I am sure, will gladly afford you any assistance in his power."

On this they all dismounted, the black soldiers taking the mules round to the stables by the side of the house, allowing their prisoners to follow the young lady into the interior. She led them into a large airy room, covered with fine matting, the only furniture consisting of several cane sofas and chairs, and a long table down the centre. She then clapped her hands, and a negro servant appeared.

"He will attend on you," she said, "while I go and see that a meal is prepared for you. My father will, I hope, soon return, and will, I am sure, be glad to afford you every assistance in his power."

The negro looked at Mr Collinson with a somewhat doubtful air, but the few fragments of gold lace remaining on his coat showed him that he was an officer.

"Would monsieur like to refresh himself?" he asked. "A bath is at his service, and, pardon me, monsieur, perhaps a fresh suit of clothes would be pleasant in which to sit down to dinner."

"Indeed, thank you," answered Mr Collinson, "but I must beg you at the same time to look after my people. We all have gone through many hardships, and I dare say they will enjoy a bath and some clean clothes as much as I shall."

"Yes, yes! I will look after them," answered the negro, in French; not very good French, by-the-by, but Mr Collinson understood it. "I must, however, obey my young mistress first, and attend to you; so, if monsieur pleases, come along."

Saying this, the negro led the way out into a garden, where was a building with a marble bath, through which the water ran from a copious stream. Leaving the lieutenant, he soon returned with a supply of light clothing, such as is usually worn in that climate. The lieutenant could not help feeling, when he returned into the dining-room, that he was far more presentable than he had been before. On looking out of the window, he saw Jack and Grimshaw with the two boys, coming along laughing heartily, dressed in negro costume of shirt and trousers. Considering the heat of the weather, their clothing was ample. Though it had not a nautical cut, any one looking at them would easily have discovered that they were British seamen, as they rolled along in their usual happy-go-lucky style.

Chapter Seventeen

Mr Collinson had not been many minutes in the dining-room, when the young lady, accompanied by an elderly-looking Frenchman with white hair, entered the room.

"You are welcome, sir, to my house," he said; "and I am happy to receive you. I lately received great kindness from your countrymen, when I was in your situation, a captive in their hands, and I am thankful to have an opportunity of returning it."

Mr Collinson made a suitable reply, adding that it was a sad thing that peaceable people should be made prisoners, and inconvenienced because their nations happened to be at war.

"Yes, indeed," added the Frenchman; "but don't speak about it. It was our Emperor who set the example."

"How long ago was it since the circumstance occurred?" asked Mr Collinson.

"But a few weeks ago," answered the Frenchman; "indeed, we have only returned home about ten days. My daughter and I were on our way from France, when our vessel was captured by an English corvette, and carried into Port Royal. The captain of the English ship treated us with great kindness, as, indeed, did several of the inhabitants of the place, especially a military officer commanding a regiment there, with whom I was formerly acquainted when I was in the army. We, on that occasion, met as enemies, but we parted as friends, and I was very glad to renew my acquaintance."

The English lieutenant listened to this account with great interest.

"And what was the name of the ship by which your vessel was captured?" he asked.

"She was a corvette, I know," he answered. "Yes, yes, I remember; her name is the *Lilly*, and her captain is Mr Trevelyan."

"That was indeed a curious coincidence, for it is the ship to which I belong," said Mr Collinson.

"The captain is indeed a kind and generous man!" exclaimed the young lady with enthusiasm. "And, now I think of it, how very strange! Surely we heard of you from Colonel Lydall. They were very anxious indeed about you. Some, in truth, thought you were lost, but Miss Lydall would not believe that; yet often she was very sad. Now I understand it all."

As may be supposed, after this information, Mr Collinson had numberless questions to ask. Sometimes he was grieved at the thoughts of the anxiety Miss Lydall was suffering; at other times, he could not help feeling grateful that her affection for him was undiminished.

While they were still speaking, a handsome repast was placed on the table, brought in by several black slaves.

"We will have your people in," said the French gentleman. "You will not object to their sitting at table, for I cannot ask them to join the black slaves."

"Certainly not," said Mr Collinson; "though I do not believe they would object to that. Probably, indeed, they would be happier by themselves."

However, the Frenchman insisted that they should come in. The boys' eyes sparkled as they found themselves seated at the table, for it was seldom or never they had seen so fine a repast.

"Won't I have a good tuck-out!" said Tommy Rebow, as he eyed the viands. "In case our nigger-guards should be inclined to starve us, we may as well take in enough to last for some days."

All hands did ample justice, as may be supposed, to the repast, the black soldiers being fed, in the mean time, in another part of the house.

At length the sergeant of the party appeared at the door, and summoned his prisoners.

"I have not asked your name," said Mr Collinson, turning to his host. "I should like to remember one of whom I shall always think with gratitude."

"My name is Mouret, and my daughter's name is Adèle; but don't suppose that I shall lose sight of you. Every influence I possess with the authorities I will exert in your favour, though I fear that is not very great."

The sergeant becoming impatient, the English party had to take a hurried farewell.

"Good-bye, monsieur; much obliged for your good dinner!" cried Jack Windy, as Monsieur Mouret kindly shook him and his companions by the hand. "We will not forget you, and be sure to give you a call, if we come this way again."

The party were once more on their road.

"Here, sir, the nigger servant gave us these bundles to look after," said Jack. "They're our duds, I suppose. One is yours, sir, and the rest ours."

"Take care of them," said Mr Collinson. "They may be useful to show who we are, should there be any doubt about the matter."

They pushed on till it was dark, as fast as the negro soldiers could march, the sergeant being anxious, apparently, to make up for the time they had spent at Monsieur Mouret's house. They reached a village at length, where he told them they must stop.

"Is there an inn to which we can go?" asked Mr Collinson.

The negro grinned.

"No, monsieur," he answered; "but quarters will be assigned to you."

After being kept waiting for some time, the sergeant, who had gone away, returned, and told them to follow.

"Here's a fine place," he said, pointing to a tumbledown barn, or shed rather; "but I will see if we can get some straw, and something for supper. You will not require much, after the good dinner you enjoyed."

In vain Mr Collinson expostulated: he found, at length, that he *must* submit. The soldiers went out, and came back in a short time with some straw, which they piled up in one corner.

"Here's enough for all of us," they grunted out; "and as for food, some farina, and cold water to wash it down, is all that is allowed. If monsieur has any money, we may procure something more suitable to his taste."

When Mr Collinson told his companions what the negro soldier said, they begged that he would not submit to any imposition.

"We can do very well without any supper, or with only what the niggers bring us," answered Jack; "and maybe we shall all want it more by-and-by."

However, when the bowl of boiled corn-meal was brought, they did ample justice to it, declaring that, for once in a way, it was not such bad food, after all. Old Grim, however, grumbled considerably, especially at night, when the rats began to chase each other about the place; and the negro soldiers kept up an interrupted snore, with occasional grunts, as a variation to the music.

"I don't see why we should complain," said Bill, at length. "We're better off than we were on the raft; and, to my mind, it is not worse than being with those cut-throat looking fellows on board the privateer."

"You are always contented," answered Grimshaw. "I can make nothing out of you."

"Just for the reason that I stick to my belief that the sun is shining up above the clouds, however dark they may be over us," answered Bill.

In spite of the rats, and the snoring and grunting of the negroes, and the unpleasant odours, even Mr Collinson fell asleep, his example being followed by his companions. They were roused up by the black sergeant at daybreak, and, without any breakfast, were ordered to proceed on their journey.

"The people have given us supper and bed, and that's all they're obliged to do," said the sergeant. "We must get breakfast where we stop at."

They travelled on as on the previous day, the scenery being sometimes very picturesque—the prickly palm, and cocoa-nut trees, and numberless shrubs with long waving leaves. Sometimes thickets of the graceful bamboo lined either side of the road; but persons, when carried off as prisoners, are not generally apt to admire the beauty of the scenery. Sunshine Bill, however, was not to be put down.

"It's one way of seeing the world that I did not expect, when I left home," he remarked to Jack Windy. "I shall have many more yarns to spin, when I get back, in consequence. Now, Tommy, look out where you are going to. You have nearly brought the mule down two or three times; and the next time we get off, I must sit ahead and steer."

They brought up at another village, where the sergeant procured some messes of boiled meal, such as they had had for supper.

"If it had not been for that kind gentleman, I don't know where we should have been by this time," said Jack. "We should have been desperately hungry, I know. Howsumdever, when we are once settled, I suppose we shall be able to get sufficient grub to keep body and soul together."

At length the prisoners arrived at a wretched-looking village, though picturesquely situated with hills rising round it.

"Halt here," said the sergeant, "while I go and inquire what quarters are to be assigned to you."

"Nothing very grand," he said, with a laugh, when he returned. "Follow me!"

"Why," said Mr Collinson, "the authorities cannot think of putting us into a place like that. It is a stable!"

"Very likely; but there's only one old horse in it, and there are three stalls: you can have one, monsieur, all to yourself, and your men can have he other. What more can you desire?"

All expostulations were vain.

"Well, we must make the best of it, my lads," said Mr Collinson, walking into the place.

"There's just one thing you must remember," shouted the sergeant: "don't be playing tricks, and turning out the horse. The owner made that a bargain; and he requires shelter as much as you do."

"Well, well!" answered the English lieutenant; "complaining is beneath us."

"We shall not do badly, sir," observed Jack, as he surveyed the place; "we don't, however, like it for you, sir; but we will get some straw and some planks, and make it as comfortable-like as we can and rig up a table. It's a shame, that it is, to turn a British officer into such a place; and the next time we get alongside a French man-of-war, in the *Lilly*, won't we give it her, that's all!"

"I hope, my lads, we may have the opportunity before long," said the lieutenant. "I am glad you take things so well. Perhaps they will mend. It's a compliment, I suspect, they pay us, to bring us here; for they have heard of the way English sailors have made their escape from prison, so they consider it is necessary to carry us all this distance from the coast."

It was nearly dark when they arrived, so that they had not much time to get their habitation in order. The night passed quietly enough, except that they were startled, every now and then, by the asthmatic cough of the horse, the croaking of the bull-frogs in a neighbouring pond, and the sound of the sentry's musket, as he grounded it every now and then, when he halted, after pacing up and down in front of the hut. Bill was awoke by hearing a voice shouting—

"Hillo, shipmates, ahoy! Where are they, blacky? What! In there? Then they are as bad off as we are."

Bill jumped up, and went to the door. There he saw an English sailor, who was, however, a stranger to him.

"Hillo! Boy," said the sailor, "what cheer? What has brought you here?"

Bill told him what had occurred.

"Well, we heard of some fresh arrivals, so I came along to see who you were. We have had nearly two score of Englishmen here, officers and men; some privateersmen, some merchant seamen, the men-of-war's men having been taken mostly in prizes, except a dozen of us who belong to the *Buzzard* schooner, and we should not have been taken had not the sloop of war we were engaging knocked away our fore-topmast, and pretty well killed or wounded two-thirds of our ship's company. Some of them, howsumdever, have been exchanged, and some have died; so that there are only a few of us remaining to make you welcome."

In a short time, the rest of the Englishmen came to greet the newcomers. One was a lieutenant, whose thin, careworn countenance showed suffering and anxiety; and another was a grey-haired old mate, who evidently cared very little what might become of him. The account they gave of their treatment was far from satisfactory.

"We receive scarcely sufficient food to keep life in us," observed the lieutenant.

All had similar complaints to make. Several days passed by, and Mr Collinson found that his countrymen had ample reason for the complaints they made.

Chapter Eighteen

Mr Collinson had expected to hear from Monsieur Mouret, but day after day passed by and no news reached him. The other lieutenant, Mr Mason, at length proposed that they should endeavour to make their escape to the coast.

"I fear that the undertaking is too hazardous to be attempted," answered Mr Collinson. "Even should we reach the coast, we may find no vessel to take us on board."

Still, as he thought over the matter, he felt greatly inclined, at all risks, to make the attempt. He had husbanded the small sum of money he possessed, in case of dire necessity, either to help them to escape or to obtain food. Meantime, the rest of the party, who had scarcely recovered from their previous hardships, were growing thinner and thinner.

Sunshine Bill was the only one who kept up his spirits. In a neighbouring cottage, to which the stable belonged, lived an old negress, the wife of the proprietor. More than once she had caught sight of Bill, who used to go outside their habitation in the evening, and amuse the rest of the party, by showing that he had not forgotten Jack Windy's instructions in dancing the hornpipe. Jack declared that he had neither strength nor inclination to shake a leg himself, but he would not mind singing a tune for Bill to dance; and dance Bill did with great glee. He did his best to try and persuade Tommy to join him, but Tommy was too weak and ill to do anything of the sort. At length, one evening, when Bill had just finished his performance, the old black woman was seen approaching with a steaming bowl in her arms.

"Dare, brave *garçon*," she said, patting Bill on the head, and pointing to the bowl, and making signs for him to eat.

She then signified that the rest might have what he chose to leave. Bill was for giving it to them at once, but she snatched the bowl back again, and squatted herself down upon the ground to see that he took enough. Whenever he stopped, she insisted upon his going on again, till at last he put his hands before him, and made signs that he could eat no more. She then allowed him to give the remainder to his hungry companions, who very soon finished it.

"Thank you, mammy," said Bill; "but, I say, could you not just bring a plate for our officer? He is as hungry as we are. He is inside there, very ill;" and Bill made signs which could scarcely be mistaken.

The old woman caught the word "officer," and she nodded her head. She soon returned with another dish of meat and vegetables, which Bill took in to Mr Collinson.

The next day after Bill had danced his hornpipe, old Mammy Otello, as they called her, came with her usual bowl of food, but on this occasion she brought a basket with various fruits besides. This she did for two or three days. One day, however, she came at an earlier hour, and made signs to Bill that he must come over to her house. The rest of the party offered to accompany him, but she very significantly showed that she did not want their society. Bill went on, wondering what she could require, though from her good-natured looks, he felt sure she intended him no harm.

As they were going towards the house, he saw a number of black people in gay dresses coming towards it from various quarters; and when he got there, he found a large room almost full of negroes in ruffles and shirt frills, and negresses in the gayest of gay gowns, somewhat scanty over the shoulder, and fitting rather close to the figure. Bill found that there was to be a black ball. At one end of the room sat, perched up on the top of a cask, a fiddler, who began scraping away as he entered.

The guests were beginning to stand up for dancing, but Mammy Otello, taking Bill by the hand, led him up to the musician, and made him understand that he was to describe the tune he wanted to have played. Bill sung out his tune as well as he could, and the fiddler made violent attempts to imitate it. At length he succeeded to his own satisfaction, if not to Bill's.

Mammy then led him back into the middle of the room, and made him understand that he was to commence dancing.

"Well, you have been a kind old soul to us," he observed; "the only one who has shown us any attention in this place; and I will do my best to please you."

The musician began to play, and Bill began to dance, and very soon the former seemed to understand exactly the sort of music required, and off he went. The guests shouted and shrieked, and clapped their hands; and the fiddler went on playing, and Bill went on dancing, and it seemed a great question which would first grow tired.

"I'll do it, that I will," thought Bill to himself; "if it's only to see these blackamoors grinning, and rolling their eyes, and shrieking, and clapping their hands in the funny way they do."

At length, so eager did the spectators become, that they pressed closer and closer upon the dancer, and Mammy Otello had to rush in and shove them back with her stout arms to prevent him from being overwhelmed.

"Tired yet, old fellow?" shouted Bill, as he went on shuffling away and kicking his heels; "I am not, let me tell you!"

The fiddler, although he might not have understood the words, comprehended the gesture, and continued working away till it seemed as if either his head or his arms and fiddle would part company, flying off in different directions. Still Bill danced, and the black fiddler played, roars of applause proceeding from the thick lips of the dark-skinned audience.

At length, Mammy Otello, fancying that Bill himself would come to pieces, or that he would fall down exhausted, rushed in, and seizing him in her arms, carried him to a seat, amid the laughter and shouting and grinning and stamping of all present; the fiddler, dropping down his right hand, and letting his instrument slip from his chin, gave vent to a loud gasp, as if he could not either have continued his exertions many seconds longer.

Bill wanted to go back for his friends, to bring them up to see the fun, but his hostess would not hear of it; and, whenever he got up to beat a retreat, she ran and brought him back again. Meantime, the room was occupied by the negroes, who danced away in a fashion Bill had never seen before.

They bowed and scraped, and set to each other, however, with all the dignity of high-bred persons. At length Bill watched his opportunity and while Mammy Otello had gone to another part of the room, he bolted out of the house, and set off as fast as his legs could carry him to his companions in captivity.

"I told you, Bill, that hornpipe of yours would gain friends wherever you go," said Jack. "I wish the old lady would give me a chance, however. Perhaps she will now be civil to us on your account."

The next day, when Mammy Otello came, she seemed rather inclined to scold Bill for running away. He got Mr Collinson to explain that he would not have done so had the rest of the party been invited, as he did no think it fair to enjoy all the fun by himself.

"Bon garçon; bon garçon!" said Mammy Otello. "The next time, for his sake, we will invite you all."

Mr Collinson was surprised, after the many promises of assistance made by Monsieur Mouret, the planter, that he should neither have seen nor heard anything of him. At length one day, a black, dressed in livery, rode into the village, inquiring for the English lieutenant who had last come. On seeing Mr Collinson, he presented a note in a lady's hand. It contained but a few words. It was from Mademoiselle Mouret.

"The day after you came here," she said, "my father was taken ill, just as he was about to set off to Point a Petre, to make interest for you. I watched over him for some days, and I confess that my grief allowed the promises he had made to escape my memory. Alas! He has been taken from me, while I myself have barely escaped with life; and only now am I sufficiently recovered to write. Fearing that you will receive very uncourteous treatment from my countrymen, and that you may be even suffering from want of food, I have sent you some provisions by our faithful servant Pierre, as also a purse, which, I trust, you will accept from one who, though in affliction, is grateful for the kindness she has received from your friends."

Mr Collinson felt that he had no right to refuse the gift which the young lady had so liberally sent. When Jack Windy heard of it, he exclaimed—

"They're all alike! Never mind whether they're French, or Dons, or blackamoors, there's a tender place in most women's hearts, unless they're downright bad, and then stand clear of them, I say, for they're worse than us men."

The next time Mammy Otello appeared, Mr Collinson placed a gold piece in her hand.

"Here, madame," he said; "I beg that you will accept this as a mark of how sensible we are of your kindness; and I beg to assure you, that, if you can give us better accommodation, we will gladly pay for it."

Mammy Otello's countenance beamed, her mouth grew considerably wider, and her eyes sparkled, partly at the sight of the money, and partly at the lieutenant's polite speech. Putting the coin into her pocket, she hastened away. In a short time she returned.

"Our family is a small one," she said; "and as the authorities here do not object, my good man and I have arranged to give you two rooms in our house, while you shall take your meals in our public room."

Mr Collinson's great difficulty was to find paper and pen to write a suitable reply to Mademoiselle Mouret. His own pocket-book had been destroyed. Not a particle of paper could he find in the place, not even the fly-leaf of a book. The other two officers had no paper of any sort. He was able, therefore, only to return a verbal answer to the young lady.

"I told you so," said Bill, when these satisfactory arrangements had been made, "that things would improve with us, and so they have."

"Yes; but we've not had yellow Jack among us yet; and depend upon it he will be coming before long," answered old Grim.

The good fortune of the Lillys, as the other prisoners called Mr Collinson and his followers, rather excited their jealousy. It tended, however, but little to raise his spirits, and he began to fear that he should never again see his friends.

"Cheer up, sir," said Bill, who had constituted himself his special attendant, "things have mended, and they will mend still more. It's a dark day when the sun does not shine out; and depend upon it, though the clouds seem pretty heavy just now, the sun will come out before long."

One day there was an unusual commotion in the village. The negroes were running about and talking to each other, and the white people especially wore anxious countenances. Soon afterwards, drums were heard, and a regiment of militia marched by. For some time, the prisoners could not ascertain what was taking place, though it was evident that something of importance was about to occur. The few regulars in the neighbourhood were seen hurriedly to march away.

Mr Collinson and the other two officers were talking together.

"Hark!" said the former; "that's the sound of a heavy gun!"

Others followed. Eagerly they listened. Some thought that they were fired at sea, others on shore. At length the excitement of the people, who had also heard the firing, greatly increased, and they confessed that an English force had come off the island, and that the English troops had landed that morning.

"I wish we could manage to get to the top of some hill to see what is going forward," exclaimed Jack Windy. "Bill, what do you say? We could get away from these fellows now."

"If Mr Collinson wishes it, I am ready enough to go," answered Bill.

"I am afraid he would say no, if we were to ask him," said Jack. "I would give anything to find out who is winning the day."

However, the nearest hills were some way off, and, even if they had got to the top of them, they could not at all tell that they would be able to see what was taking place. The sound of the firing increased, and it became very certain that a fierce engagement was going on. The people about them, however, knew no more than they did, so they could gain no information.

At length a body of men was seen coming over a pass in the distance. They were watched anxiously. Who could they be—English or French? On they came, increasing their speed. As they drew nearer, it was evident that they were black troops—the same regiment, indeed, which had passed through the village in the morning. It seemed, from the way they marched, or rather ran, that they thought an enemy was behind them. They bore among them several wounded men. Not till they had hurried through the village did they halt.

At first, no one would say what had happened. The hopes of the English prisoners, however, began to rise, and soon the news spread through the village that a fierce battle had been fought, and that the English had been victorious. At length a French officer was seen coming along the road, who stopped for a few minutes to give his horse some water. Mr Collinson approached him.

"I am one of the English officers who have been some time prisoners in the island," he said, addressing him in French.

"Ah!" he answered, "you need consider yourselves prisoners no longer. Your countrymen have come with an overwhelming force and taken possession of the island. I am sent with despatches to the other side, to give notice of the capitulation."

This news rapidly spread throughout the village.

A loud cheer burst from Jack and the boys' throats, in which even Grimshaw joined.

The other prisoners came hurrying up to hear the news, and three more hearty cheers were given, in which even many of the negroes for sympathy could not help joining. There, whites and blacks were shouting together, and shaking hands cordially.

There was some difficulty in getting conveyances for the whole party. At length, however, mules and horses sufficient to carry them were collected. Mammy Otello gave Bill an affectionate embrace, as he wished her good-bye, an honour she did not bestow on the rest of the party. She insisted, however, on their taking several delicacies of her own cooking; and, at length, all hands being under weigh, with repeated cheers, the sailors set out from the place of their long imprisonment.

Mr Collinson stopped at the house where they had been entertained on their way. Mademoiselle Mouret entreated him not to thank her for the trifle she had sent, and begged him to assure his friends that, should they ever come to the island, it would be her pride and pleasure to receive them.

On arriving in sight of the sea, a large fleet of men-of-war and transports were seen below them, while British troops lay encamped on the side of the hill. Having been delivered over by the French authorities, in due form, to the English, they once more had the satisfaction of feeling themselves free men. Among the ships lay a fine corvette. No sooner did Jack Windy's eye fall on her than he exclaimed—

"She's the *Lilly* herself, or I'm a Dutchman!"

Hastening down to the port, they eagerly put off in the first boats they could find. As they pulled alongside, none on board knew them. Captain Trevelyan and the other officers were on deck. Besides Mr Barker, there was another lieutenant.

"Then they must suppose I am lost," thought Mr Collinson, as he stepped aft. "I am afraid I am not known," he said.

Captain Trevelyan started. A beam of pleasure lighted up his face.

Fortunately, the corvette was immediately despatched with news of the capture of the island. She had a quick passage to Jamaica, and Mr Collinson lost not many hours, after his arrival, in hurrying to Uphill Cottage. The black cook told Bill, who went up with him on his next visit, that the young lady did not go into hysterics at the sight of him, but, although she had been somewhat sad and pale before, her colour returned, and her voice was as cheerful and merry as it used to be. As Mr Collinson had been superseded, he did not return to the *Lilly*; indeed, a few days after her arrival, he received his promotion.

"Now he is a commander, I suppose he will be marrying Miss Lydall," observed Bill—a remark the sagacity of which was proved a few days before the *Lilly* sailed for England, where Mr and Mrs Collinson soon after arrived in a merchant-vessel.

Although Bill did not bring home as much gold as he had expected, he was received not the less warmly by widow Sunnyside and his brothers and sisters. Soon afterwards, Captain Collinson called at the widow's house, and left with her a roll of gold pieces.

"Here are Bill's wages," he said. "He attended me as my servant, and I consider them justly his due; indeed," he added, "if it had not been for his hopeful and cheerful spirit, I believe that I should have sunk under the hardships we had to go through."

The next time Captain Trevelyan went to sea, he took Sunshine Bill with him; indeed, for many years he served either with him, or with Captain Collinson, whose coxswain he became. At that time, finding an honest girl who reminded him of his happy little mother, he married, and had no reason to repent his choice. Ultimately, having improved in his education, he passed as a boatswain, in which capacity he served for many years, till he was laid up, like many another noble tar, in ordinary; but to the end of his days he maintained the same cheerful and hopeful disposition which had carried him through so many trials in his youth—a disposition which was happily inherited by a numerous offspring.